THE WORLD'S WIFE

CAROL ANN DUFFY

NOTES BY MARY GREEN

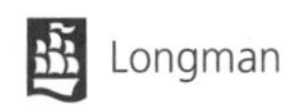

YORK PRESS
322 Old Brompton Road, London SW5 9JH

PEARSON EDUCATION LIMITED
Edinburgh Gate, Harlow,
Essex CM20 2JE, United Kingdom
Associated companies, branches and representatives throughout the world

First published 2007
Third impression 2008

ISBN 978-1-4058-6185-4

Phototypeset by Pantek Arts Ltd, Maidstone, Kent
Printed in China

Contents

Part One
Introduction

Part Two
The text

INTRODUCTION

HOW TO STUDY A POEM

Studying on your own requires self-discipline and a carefully thought-out work plan in order to be effective.

- Poetry is the most challenging kind of literary writing. In your first reading you may well not understand what the poem is about. Don't jump too swiftly to any conclusions about the poem's meaning.
- Read the poem many times, and including out loud. After the second or third reading, write down any features you find interesting or unusual.
- What is the poem's tone of voice? What is the poem's mood?
- Does the poem have an argument? Is it descriptive?
- Is the poet writing in his or her own voice? Might he or she be using a **persona** or mask?
- Is there anything special about the kind of language the poet has chosen? Which words stand out? Why?
- What elements are repeated? Consider **alliteration**, **assonance**, rhyme, rhythm, **metaphor** and ideas.
- What might the poem's images suggest or **symbolise**?
- What might be significant about the way the poem is arranged in lines? Is there a regular pattern of lines? Does the grammar coincide with the ending of the lines or does it 'run over'? What is the effect of this?
- Do not consider the poem in isolation. Can you compare and contrast the poem with any other work by the same poet or with any other poem that deals with the same theme?
- What do you think the poem is about?
- Every argument you make about the poem must be backed up with details and quotations that explore its language and organisation.
- Always express your ideas in your own words.

These York Notes offer an introduction to *The World's Wife* and cannot substitute for close reading of the text and the study of secondary sources.

CONTEXT

The word 'poetry' comes from the Greek word *poesis*, meaning 'making' or 'creating'. People have been writing poetry for thousands of years – the earliest we have dates back to c.3000BC.

READING *THE WORLD'S WIFE*

The World's Wife was first published in 1999 and is the work of a prolific and well-established poet. Carol Ann Duffy had already been involved in many artistic projects (see **Chronology**) and had published several notable volumes of poetry before *The World's Wife*, including *Standing Female Nude* (1985), *Selling Manhattan* (1987) and *Mean Time* (1993), all to critical acclaim.

In her poetic works, Duffy explores many themes: politics, particularly **gender politics**, sexual identity, love, time and loss, the nature of language and also religion from the perspective of a non-believer who was raised a Catholic. Her development as an artist can be traced from her early work, which began in her teens, through to her mature work, where she frequently uses the **dramatic monologue**. Prior to this, in such volumes as *Fifth Last Song* (1982), the emphasis was on **lyric** poetry. The dramatic monologue, however, allows the poet to **foreground** the voice or voices to create a strong presence, so that we feel a person other than the poet is addressing us directly. This allows Duffy to pursue what seems to be one of her major concerns: to give a voice to those in society who are not usually heard (see **Poetic forms: The dramatic monologue**). As she has matured, these voices have become increasingly female. *The World's Wife* is an example of this. Duffy has commented in an interview with Peter Forbes that she is unlikely to write poetry in the male voice again ('Winning Lines', published in the *Guardian* on 31 August 2002).

CHECK THE BOOK

An example of the dramatic monologue in Duffy's earlier work is 'Havisham' (the Miss Havisham of Charles Dickens' *Great Expectations*) in *Mean Time.*

Not only are all the voices in *The World's Wife* those of female speakers, but every poem in the collection is a dramatic monologue. Each poem, of which there are thirty, has a single speaker. Even 'The Kray Sisters' can be regarded as a monologue, since the twins speak as one voice. Neither addresses the reader separately. The 'wife' of the title represents the wives of famous men, be they real, fictional, mythic or biblical, while the common saying 'the world and his wife' is altered to give the emphasis to the wife. Rather than focus on the **personified** male 'world', as the saying does, the poet subverts it, giving it an **ironic** twist. It is the wives' voices that will be heard in these poems, signalling that the female is not an adjunct to the male. The tone of the title could also be read to suggest

CHECK THE BOOK

For an accessible and well-written study see *Carol Ann Duffy* by Deryn Rees-Jones (2001).

'world-weariness' in the sense of being tired of a male-dominated world. We can almost hear a knowing sigh from the long-suffering collective wife. Some of the poems clearly reinforce this tone: 'he could bore for Purgatory. He was small, / didn't prepossess. So he tried to impress', declares Mrs Aesop (1–2), who endures her husband's homilies ad nauseam.

Many of the wives in this collection may be long-suffering, but they are certainly not victims. They are sardonic, angry, cruel and impatient; and occasionally, like Anne Hathaway, they are joyful. In certain poems – 'Anne Hathaway' is one – the female speaker retains her own name, usually because she is unmarried or a character from mythology. But where they are wives, some reference is usually made to their married state. 'Anne Hathaway' is an exception in this respect, since the poet is also celebrating Shakespeare's language. Nor is Duffy afraid to tackle controversial areas. Her women are by no means virtuous. Salome, for example, is depicted as a serial killer, and Myra Hindley the Moors Murderer as 'the Devil's wife' in the poem of that name.

The volume also has elegance. This multiplicity of female voices lies between 'Little Red-Cap', the first poem, and 'Demeter', the last poem. In these two poems the speakers are, respectively, an adolescent girl at a time of sexual awakening and self-affirmation, and a mature woman and mother. In this last poem, Demeter's daughter, Persephone, enters. She, like Little Red-Cap, represents renewal and reaffirms the female spirit. The volume therefore comes full circle.

The World's Wife is, for the most part, satiric, witty and playful. The poet is concerned to debunk the male persona attached to such grandees as Sigmund Freud or Charles Darwin. This does not mean that Duffy condemns these thinkers or their work, though she may or may not agree with them. She seeks to highlight the way in which women in general have been at best ignored and at worst silenced down the ages; women who have been and who in different walks of life still are part of a system that assumes they are defined by their male partners, while they themselves remain in the shadows. This silencing runs deep, so it is no surprise that figures from myths and fairy tales are also included in the volume. These are archetypal

CONTEXT

Duffy has written picture books for children, including *Another Night Before Christmas* (2005), which retells a Victorian tale by Clement Moore.

CHECK THE BOOK

The criminal mind is explored elsewhere by Duffy in her poem 'Psychopath' (*Selling Manhattan*).

figures whose psychological effect is profound (see **The power of the tale**). Duffy is attacking, albeit **satirically**, a social system in which the male world holds most of the power. Recognising that this *is* a social system reminds us that men themselves are caught up or **socialised** into it, which in turn prevents a simplistic reading of the text as merely attacking all men per se.

In *The World's Wife* Duffy is closely linked to a tradition of female writers. She is almost certainly familiar with the work of the novelist and short-story writer Angela Carter (1940–92), as well as the poets Anne Sexton (1928–74) and Liz Lochhead (b.1947), all of whom are **revisionist** writers of the fairy tale. She must also have read Jackie Kay (b.1961), with whom she lived for several years. One of her main influences is Adrienne Rich (b.1929), a radical **feminist** and lesbian poet whose volume *The Dream of a Common Language: Poems 1974–1977* (1978) is concerned with the female writing identity. We can also feel the influence of Sylvia Plath (1932–63) in Duffy's use of stark images and sudden pauses. Robert Browning (1812–89) is another likely influence. He is well known for his use of the **dramatic monologue**, as is the modernist poet and critic T. S. Eliot (1888–1965), acknowledged to be one of her greatest influences. Her early writing would have been influenced by the Liverpool poets, of whom her friend Adrian Henri (1932–2000) was part; and as a very young poet she is reputed to have experimented with the style of the Romantic poet John Keats (1795–1821), whose poetry is marked by rich language and intense images.

Carol Ann Duffy has become one of the leading poets of the day. Much of her work is accessible and easily engages the reader, but she also explores complex areas of human experience. This dual aspect of her work is what makes *The World's Wife* an enjoyable and rewarding collection to study.

CHECK THE NET

For more information about John Keats, Robert Browning and T. S. Eliot, together with online versions of their poetry, go to **www.online-literature.com**

CONTEXT

Romanticism is a term used to describe the philosophical and literary movement dating from the French Revolution (1789) to *c.*1830. Central to it is the importance of the imagination, the individual and nature as a source of moral knowledge. Other well-known Romantic writers were William Wordsworth (1770–1850), Samuel Taylor Coleridge (1772–1834), Percy Bysshe Shelley (1792–1822) and Lord Byron (1788–1824).

PART TWO

THE TEXT

NOTE ON THE TEXT

The World's Wife was first published by Picador in 1999. A paperback edition by the same publisher was released in 2000 and is used in these Notes. Some of the poems appeared in other collections (such as the anthology *After Ovid: New Metamorphoses* in 1994, and *The Pamphlet* in 1998) and magazines, including the *Poetry Review*, the *New Statesman* and the *Guardian*, before being published as a collection.

DETAILED SUMMARIES

LITTLE RED-CAP

- Little Red-Cap has reached adolescence and meets a wolf in the woods.
- The poem explores her subsequent life with him and her rejection of him.

This rewriting of the fairy tale 'Little Red-Cap' or 'Little Red Riding Hood' explores the sexual awakening of the girl of the original tale, who, in Duffy's version, is an adolescent and a burgeoning poet. She willingly loses her virginity to the wolf, an older established poet, and the poem charts the relationship from enchantment, through disaffection, to violent rejection.

COMMENTARY

The first words of the poem, 'At childhood's end', signal adolescence. Little Red-Cap no longer wishes to be saved by the huntsman and is already aware of the male world and its erotic desires, in which a woman may have power: 'allotments / kept, like mistresses, by kneeling married men' (2–3). She wants to be free of the mundane suburban streets, playing fields and factories to explore the unknown at 'the edge of the woods' (5).

CONTEXT

The original source of this fairy tale is Charles Perrault's 'Le Petit Chaperon rouge' ('Little Red Riding Hood') published in 1697, in which the child is eaten. A moral in verse, on the virtues of obedience, accompanies the tale. A new version, 'Rotkäppchen' ('Little Red-Cap'), appeared in the Brothers Grimm collection in 1812. Tales were often rewritten to suit the social conventions of the time; the Brothers Grimm revised many fairy tales, as have other writers.

CONTEXT

Roland Barthes (1915–80), a French philosopher, critic and **post-structuralist**, wrote *Le Plaisir du texte* (*The Pleasure of the Text*) in 1973. In it he explores the liberating playfulness of language. The text for Barthes has no fixed meanings because meaning in language is unstable. The reader can engage with the writer by losing himself or herself in the text. This loss of self is the high point of pleasure.

CHECK THE FILM

The Company of Wolves (1984), directed by Neil Jordan, is the film of the short story of the same name by Angela Carter published in her collection *The Bloody Chamber and Other Stories* (1979). It is a rewriting of 'Little Red Riding Hood'.

The early lines of this **sestet** have a rhythm that matches the images. It is flat, slow, sombre, like the 'silent railway line' (4), until the **end stop** after 'woods' (5), when Little Red-Cap's interest is aroused by the sight of the wolf. From then on, the poem gains speed. It is accentuated by **internal rhymes** – 'drawl … paw … jaw' (8–9) – as the wolf-poet reads his verse at the poetry reading, where Little Red-Cap wastes no time in trapping him, a reversal of the fairy-tale plot. Duffy effectively exploits the saying 'Sweet sixteen and never been kissed', replacing 'kissed' with other images so that the last line of the second **stanza** rushes with excitement into the third.

Why is Little Red-Cap so interested in an older man? 'Poetry', we are told (13). She wants not only 'scraps of red' (17), a **metaphor** for sexual experience, but to be initiated into poetry, its mystique and power – that 'dark tangled thorny place' (15) – and to learn wisdom through 'the eyes of owls' (16). She wants to know the pleasure of the text – a theory of which Duffy, with her background in philosophy and **semiotics**, would be aware.

But Little Red-Cap is vulnerable. In the woods she leaves behind 'stockings ripped to shreds' (17), 'murder clues' (18) reminiscent of the victims of child molesters. By the fourth stanza, she has entered the wolf's lair. The staccato chant in the first line, 'got there, wolf's lair, better beware', is a warning (19). It is also a reminder of playground rhymes, and has undertones of the sinister old game 'What's the time, Mr Wolf?' When Little Red-Cap goes in search of 'a living bird – white dove –' (24), a metaphor for her own poetic voice, it is gobbled up in 'One bite, dead' by the wolf: 'How nice, breakfast in bed, he said' (26). Not only has her potential mentor devoured her poetic voice, but 'breakfast in bed' suggests that she has already been forced into the female domestic role and finds herself powerless. Her only sustenance is the wolf's books, in which she finds 'warm, beating, frantic, winged' words (30). There is 'music' here, too, but also 'blood', and the bird seems trapped or caged. The image of the bird as her own poetic voice is repeated throughout the poem.

Only after ten years in the wolf's lair does experience teach Little Red-Cap that nothing will change. She is now a grown woman, but her poetry, her self-expression, will never be properly heard. The metaphor for this living death is violent – 'a mushroom / stoppers the mouth of a buried corpse' (32–3) – but also rhythmically monotonous, as though spoken between clenched teeth, and is followed by a cynical assessment of the 'greying wolf' who 'howls the same old song at the moon, year in, year out' (34–5). Again we hear the weary, flat rhythm of the first stanza. Finally Little Red-Cap becomes desperate. The **caesura** in the middle of line 36 increases the tension as she is engulfed by fury: 'I took an axe'. The **enjambment** takes the reader into the last stanza, in which Little Red-Cap splits open the wolf, 'scrotum to throat' (39). It is a cathartic deliverance. Revealed are her 'grandmother's bones' (40), a link to the matriarch and the female line. Released from her stultifying existence, Little Red-Cap has found her own voice, like the bird, 'singing', and is free to leave the forest in splendid isolation.

CHECK THE BOOK

For a very useful discussion, see Avril Horner's essay '"Small Female Skull": patriarchy and philosophy in the poetry of Carol Ann Duffy' in *The Poetry of Carol Ann Duffy: 'Choosing Tough Words'*, edited by Angelica Michelis and Antony Rowland (2003). Horner makes links between the burgeoning female poet, Little Red-Cap, and Sylvia Plath's female speaker in her poem 'The Colossus'. The Colossus, Horner notes, represents 'the male world of poetry' (p. 110).

THETIS

- Thetis, a sea nymph, escapes from her suitor by continually changing shape.
- Eventually she marries him, and the poem culminates with the birth of a child.

In this poem Duffy portrays the sea nymph Thetis as a woman escaping the clutches of a powerful and violent man. Thetis uses her wits, changing shape each time she is caught, until eventually she succumbs, marries her suitor and changes again at the birth of her child.

COMMENTARY

Thetis is a nereid or sea nymph goddess of Greek mythology, one of the daughters of Nereus the Titan and Old Man of the Sea. Pursued by Zeus, the ruler of the gods, and by Poseidon, the sea god, Thetis is promised to the mortal Peleus after the Fates declare that she will give birth to a child who will be greater than his father. The child is Achilles, the hero in Homer's *Iliad*. Like her father, Thetis has the power of metamorphosis.

CONTEXT

The Fates in Greek mythology govern the destinies of all livings things, by a mystical thread. The first, Clotho, spins the thread; the second, Lachesis, measures its length and thus the length of a life; the third, Atropos, severs it when a life is to cease.

CONTEXT

The Rime of the Ancient Mariner (1798) is a **narrative** poem written by Samuel Taylor Coleridge (1772–1834) and was first published in *Lyrical Ballads*. The mariner, who is also the storyteller, slays an albatross, a bird of good omen, and brings catastrophe to the crew.

CHECK THE BOOK

In Robert Graves' *The Greek Myths* (1955), Thetis transforms herself into 'fire, water, a lion, a serpent' and a huge cuttlefish to escape Peleus.

CHECK THE BOOK

Jeffrey Wainwright suggests that Thetis' 'joy [at the birth of her son] will be limited by loss: the failure of Thetis finally to protect her son' ('Female metamorphoses: Carol Ann Duffy's Ovid' in *The Poetry of Carol Ann Duffy: 'Choosing Tough Words'* by Angelica Michelis and Antony Rowland, 2003, p. 55).

In the poem the suitor is never mentioned, but his presence is constantly felt in his determined pursuit of Thetis, who is a **metaphor** both for women's vulnerability at the hands of men, and for their capacity to survive and adapt. In the first verse, as a bird 'in the hand / of a man' (2–3), she can be crushed by 'the squeeze of his fist' (6), so she transforms herself, becoming in the second verse a great albatross. The Christian image of suffering on the Cross and the reference to Coleridge's poem *The Rime of the Ancient Mariner*, in which an albatross is slain by a crossbow, dominate the verse: 'Then I did this: / shouldered the cross of an albatross' (7–8). Thetis' burden is twofold. As Thetis transformed into an albatross, her wings are clipped and she is powerless. But as Thetis the woman she must also carry the bird, 'the cross of an albatross', like the cursed mariner who must wear the bird around his neck as the price for slaying it. In her next **transformation** Thetis becomes a snake, but her efforts work no better, for she feels 'the grasp of his strangler's clasp' (17) and must transform herself once more. There is also a **double entendre** in the verse. As well as a reference to shape-shifting, the word 'shape' is a flippant comment on the modern woman's preoccupation with body weight and size: 'Size 8. Snake. / Big Mistake' (14–15).

Typically, the poet draws on a wide range of language. The theme of metamorphosis allows Duffy to explore female transcendence, a common theme in women's poetry. Throughout 'Thetis' Duffy takes certain elements of the tale and weaves her own images, while following the mythical narrative. Thetis becomes variously a lion: 'roar, claw, 50 lb paw' (19), sea creatures: 'Mermaid, me, big fish, eel, dolphin, / whale' (27–8), and 'racoon, skunk, stoat, / … weasel, ferret, bat, mink, rat' (32–3); but in each case she is unable to escape fully, until as 'wind' and 'hurricane' she is shot down by 'a fighter plane' (verse 7). Becoming fire, she is consumed by passion and succumbs to her suitor. As the groom, however, wears 'asbestos' (45), he seems impervious to her 'tongue' of 'flame' and her 'kisses' that 'burned' (43–4). Finally Thetis is transformed once more through the birth of her child. It is the birth of Achilles, a triumphant birth.

We can interpret the last lines of the poem in various ways. We could argue that Thetis as a mother undergoes a different kind of transformation; moreover, as a mother of a boy child her attitude to masculinity is tempered by mother love. She is, after all, 'turned inside out' (47), which suggests a full and complete change. In the myth Thetis is highly protective of her son, attempting to make him immortal.

Written in eight **sestets**, the movement of the poem is carefully controlled **free verse**. The rhythm is irregular, but there are many rhymes. Sometimes these are simple **end rhymes**: 'man … sang' and 'sky … eye' appear in the first two verses, or often a combination of rhymes is used. The fifth verse is littered with these. There are **internal rhymes**, 'roar, claw' (19), repeated as end rhymes: 'paw', 'raw', 'gore', 'jaw' and so on. This excess of rhyme could create a comic effect, but instead it creates speed. Similarly the **run-on lines** used – for example 'I changed my tune / to racoon, skunk' (31–2) – carry the idea from one line to another, and hurry the poem along. But there are also abrupt pauses, occurring at the end of lines and within them: 'Then I did this: / shouldered the cross … the sky. / Why? To follow a ship' (7–10). The overall effect of these poetic techniques creates the impression of a creature at once fast-moving but also on the lookout for danger, ready to shift course. Knowing that Thetis is a sea nymph creates an image in the mind's eye of a slippery, darting fish.

CONTEXT

In the *Iliad*, an epic poem written in twenty-four books by the ancient Greek poet Homer, the great warrior Achilles is killed by Paris from an arrow to the heel. Thetis, in her attempt to protect her son against death, had dipped him in the waters of the River Styx as a baby, but failed to cover the heel where she held him, hence the term 'Achilles heel', meaning a fatal weakness.

GLOSSARY

34 **taxidermist** person who cleans and stuffs dead animal specimens

35 **formaldehyde** a poisonous gas used as a preservative for specimens

45 **asbestos** a non-burning heat-resistant material

QUEEN HEROD

- Queen Herod welcomes the three Queens to the palace.
- They bring gifts for the newly born girl child, and Queen Herod swears to protect her daughter from male exploitation.
- She orders the deaths of all sons.

CONTEXT

Matthew is the only gospel that records Herod's infanticide (Chapter 2). In Christian tradition it is known as the Massacre of the Innocents. Herod learns of the birth of Jesus from the three wise men, and asks them to tell him the location when they have found the child, so that he can worship the baby. But the Magi are warned in a dream not to return to Herod, and instead return home via another route.

CONTEXT

In Charles Perrault's 'La Belle au bois dormant' ('Sleeping Beauty'), the good fairies bestow similar qualities on the baby Princess Aurora: beauty, wit, grace and the ability to dance, sing and play any instrument. But there will be no princely husband for Queen Herod's daughter if her mother can prevent it.

Queen Herod describes the arrival of the three wise Queens to her palace in winter. They have come bearing gifts for Queen Herod's newborn daughter. They warn her to look out for '*a star in the East*' (31) signalling the birth of a baby boy, an omen of male domination. Queen Herod fears the exploitation of her daughter and the threat to the child's female identity, and orders the deaths of all boy children.

COMMENTARY

Duffy has taken elements from the biblical gospels, revised them and woven them together to create an alternative female perspective. To follow this perspective, the original elements need to be understood. The first two elements that run through the poem are the arrival of the Magi or the three wise men at the birth of Jesus, and the star in the East signalling the birth. The third element refers to Herod's decree that all boy children of two years old and under living in Bethlehem should be put to death. According to the Gospel of Matthew, Herod feared the Old Testament prophecy that the Messiah would come. Since this would be a threat to his power, he ordered infanticide. All three elements – the wise men, the birth of Jesus and Herod's act – are part of the story of the Nativity.

The speaker is Queen Herod and the events are seen through her eyes. But the three Queens are given prominent positions, and Queen Herod reports their words in italics. The poem, written in **free verse**, opens with the arrival at the palace gates of the matriarchal 'Three Queens', an **allusion** to 'the Three Kings', the patriarchal Magi of the biblical story. The Queens are majestic and exotic, 'dressed in furs, accented' (3), and they arrive at Herod's equally exotic palace with its 'sunken baths' and 'curtained beds' (9). Once the drunken Herod has fallen asleep – Duffy quickly ushers him out of the poem here – the Queens are taken to see the new daughter in her crib. This is clearly a reference to the Nativity scene and the birth of Jesus, but the gifts given are not the traditional gold, frankincense and myrrh, but grace, strength and happiness.

The three Queens warn of calamity. A star in the East signals the birth of a male boy. The lines are heavy with **symbolism** and the meaning multifaceted. The new star *'pierced through the night like a nail'* (33) recalls Christ's Crucifixion, suffering and death. In the poem, however, the star presages suffering for the female child and, by the same token, the matriarchal line. We can assume, therefore, that the birth of the boy child represents masculinity, rather than Jesus specifically. A whole litany of male figures – *'The Husband. Hero. Hunk'* (35), *'Adulterer. Bigamist'* (37), *'The Rat'* (38) and more – are paraded before the reader's eyes by the matriarch Queens. The significance and power of the three Queens is evident when Queen Herod swears to protect her child (46–7). The black Queen of 'insolent lust' (30) takes out Queen Herod's breast in an act which is both sexual and nurturing and puts it to the baby's mouth in what seems to be an allusion to the attractions of lesbianism and the power of motherhood. Again, there are **connotations** of power and sexuality when the three Queens leave. Queen Herod watches 'each turbaned Queen / rise like a god on the back of her beast' (58–9). This is contrasted with the image of Herod. He is given no dignity. The relationship with his wife is described by her in terms of female sexual subjugation, and he appears again in the third verse as a 'fusty bulk' (61). There is no joy in the description of the lovemaking described by Queen Herod. Her experiences would seem to fuel her hatred of the masculine as the black Queen's urgent warnings of the star obsess her. She sends for 'the Chief of Staff, / a mountain man / with a red scar, like a tick' (69–71) and commands him to carry out her brutal order to murder the boy children and *'Spare not one'* (77).

Here Duffy subverts the original story. Herod's motives for the Massacre of the Innocents are replaced by his wife's. She seeks to murder the boy children because she fears the loss of female power, symbolised in her daughter's potential domination by **patriarchy**. If Herod's **narrative** is to run its course, however, the prophecy will come true. The final verses accentuate Queen Herod's anxiety that the power of the female line will indeed be lost to the male, 'blatant, brazen, buoyant in the East – / and blue – / The Boyfriend's Star' (87–9). Arguably the poet is pointing up the historical treatment of women in the Christian Church over the last two thousand years, in which gender roles have been clearly defined along patriarchal

CONTEXT

Herod the Great (*c.*74–4BC) was king of Judaea (37–4BC) under the Romans. His history is recorded by Flavius Josephus in the first century AD.

CHECK THE FILM

The Nativity Story directed by Catherine Hardwicke (2006) is a conventional retelling of the biblical tale.

CHECK THE BOOK

'Queen Herod' has parallels with T. S. Eliot's 'The Journey of the Magi' (written in 1927, and included in his *Collected Poems 1909–1962*), also a **dramatic monologue**. The depiction of winter, the demands of the journey and the exhausted camels are similarly evoked in Eliot's poem. There is also a focus on the death of an old order, and the rise of the new in Christianity.

principles and in which women have been denied positions of equal authority with men. Nonetheless, the picture presented of women in 'Queen Herod' is not one of subjugation. They are all fierce matriarchs, bold, Amazonian and as brutal as any man in the protection of their daughters and their line.

GLOSSARY

36	***Paramour*** a lover
	Je t'adore I love you
80	**Orion** constellation; in Greek mythology the giant huntsman slain by Artemis, the daughter of Zeus, and set in the sky
83	**Dog Star** Sirius, the brightest star in the sky, located in the constellation Canis Major; so called because it appears to follow the hunter Orion
85	**a studded, diamond W** refers to Cassiopeia, a constellation said to represent a vain queen in Greek mythology

MRS MIDAS

- Mrs Midas finds that everything her husband touches turns to gold.
- As the implications become clear, she realises she cannot live with her husband and the marriage comes to an end.

When Mrs Midas pauses in her kitchen to watch her husband take a pear from a tree, she is surprised to see it shine. As she gradually realises that everything her husband touches turns to gold, something he has wished for, she knows that their time together is limited. The marriage finally breaks apart, and Mrs Midas contemplates her husband's selfishness and what she has lost.

COMMENTARY

One of the best-known Greek myths is the story of King Midas. In the past it was often used as a **cautionary tale** to teach the young the dangers of avarice. We could be forgiven for thinking that Duffy does much the same here. She takes the plot and places it in a modern, middle-class suburban setting. The poem opens in a

CONTEXT

Midas was the mythical king of Phrygia, now part of Turkey, renowned for his hedonism and love of luxury.

relaxed mood. Affluent Mrs Midas is drinking a glass of wine while the evening meal gently cooks. Her husband is in their spacious garden, plucking a pear from a tree. She notices that the pear shines 'like a light bulb' (11) and wonders if he is 'putting fairy lights in the tree' (12). Duffy is having fun at the Midases' expense, largely through **irony**. Mrs Midas, unlike the reader, is unaware of how the story works out. References to their opulent, bourgeois life not only suit the myth of King Midas, but poke fun at the middle classes in general. The pear from the garden is not simply a pear, it is a 'Fondante d'Automne' (10), and the lights that Mrs Midas believes to be there are fashionably decorative.

As Mrs Midas tracks her husband's progress from the garden to the house, she begins to realise that something is amiss. Everything he touches shines; he literally has the Midas touch. With the reference to 'the Field of the Cloth of Gold' (15) we are reminded of wealth and ostentation, and in the image of Mrs Macready the love of material things. While Mrs Midas still exists within the normal world of her marriage, Midas has entered another realm: 'The look on his face was strange, wild, vain' (17). Full knowledge of what is happening only strikes her at the dinner table, when her husband attempts to drink the wine, 'a fragrant, bone-dry white from Italy' (23), and she is catapulted into action, refusing contact with him and removing the cat to a safe place. Midas has become a pariah.

In the Greek myth Dionysus (also known as Bacchus), the god of wine, and usually associated with indulgence, grants Midas his wish. Mrs Midas reflects on the shallowness and emptiness of desiring wealth for wealth's sake. She admits that 'we all have wishes; granted' (31). Duffy skilfully uses the semicolon here to show that Mrs Midas is in agreement with this view, then allows her to observe with biting humour that her husband indeed 'has wishes granted' (32). She then considers the nature of gold, with its bright seductive qualities: 'aurum, soft, untarnishable' (33). But gold is also inert and lifeless and cannot itself provide even the bare necessities of life, though she notes archly that her husband will have to give up smoking. Many of the images throughout the poem accentuate the beauty of gold – 'luteous' (35), 'honeyed embrace' (41) – while also undercutting it with humour, mainly irony, to remind us how gold has been the Midases' undoing.

CONTEXT

The Field of the Cloth of Gold was the scene of a meeting near Calais between Henry VIII of England and Francis I of France in 1520. The two monarchs were determined to outdo each other in their displays of wealth, and erected elaborate temporary palaces.

CONTEXT

In the poem Mrs Midas compares her husband's mindset to that of Mrs Macready, the housekeeper in *The Lion, the Witch and the Wardrobe* (1950) by C. S. Lewis (1898–1963). Mrs Macready values possessions above people, placing the professor's house and contents above the children who live there.

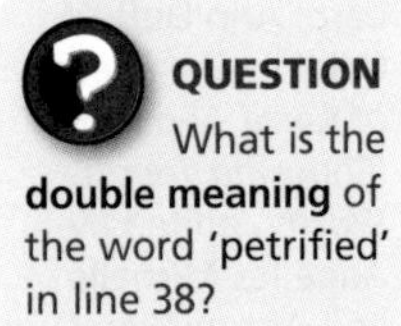

QUESTION

What is the **double meaning** of the word 'petrified' in line 38?

CHECK THE NET

The name Midas has a historic origin. Kings of this name ruled over Phrygia, now in Turkey. Archaeological remains in Gordion show a seventh-century BC burial chamber with many artefacts. Visit **www. allaboutturkey.com**

CONTEXT

'The Midas touch' has entered the language to mean the ability to make and amass money.

CHECK THE BOOK

An academic took Duffy to task for not engaging fully with the Tiresias myth, which is more complex than her poem suggests. In response Duffy humorously added '*from*' to the title. This story is recounted by Jeffrey Wainwright in his essay 'Female metamorphoses: Carol Ann Duffy's Ovid' in *The Poetry of Carol Ann Duffy: 'Choosing Tough Words'*, edited by Angelica Michelis and Antony Rowland (2003), p. 47.

As the plot runs its course, the mood shifts and we feel sympathy for Mrs Midas. She recalls how tactile and intimate she and her husband once were, 'in those halcyon days' (40). Verse eight is especially touching: Mrs Midas dreams that she bears a child of gold, a beautiful doll with 'perfect ore limbs' (45), reminding us of the human children she will never have. And thus the marriage comes to an end. She watches his decline from a safe distance. The **lyrical** nature of the images is in direct contrast with the life Midas is leading, as he becomes part of the mythical world he has helped to create (55–60).

The poem is structured in a controlled manner of eleven **sestets**, allowing each short episode to unfold. At the beginning of the last verse, when Mrs Midas contemplates all that has happened, she draws attention to her position – and the **symbolic** position of many wives. Midas, in pursuit of his own ends, forgot his wife. The final lines conjure up her need for human warmth, and we feel for her in her loneliness: 'I miss most, / even now, his hands, his warm hands on my skin, his touch' (65–6).

GLOSSARY

10	**Fondante d'Automne** a variety of high quality sweet pear
33	**aurum** Latin for 'gold'
35	**luteous** orange-yellow colour
39	**Tutankhamun** ancient Egyptian pharaoh, whose tomb was discovered in 1922 and contained magnificent riches
59	**Pan** nature god of flocks, woods and trees in Greek mythology

FROM MRS TIRESIAS

- Mrs Tiresias tells the reader that her husband has changed from a man to a woman.
- The poem describes their relationship and the effects of Tiresias' gender change.

The speaker of this poem is Mrs Tiresias, although occasionally she reports her husband's actual words. She recounts her husband's **transformation** from man to woman, and describes his defects in both sexes and the subsequent effect on their relationship after the change. Mrs Tiresias undergoes her own kind of transformation.

COMMENTARY

The startling declaration in the first few lines makes it quite clear what the focus of the poem will be: Tiresias' sudden transformation. The effect created is not simply one of being spoken to directly, which is typical of the **dramatic monologue**; the tone is confidential. Mrs Tiresias appears to be chatting to the reader, as though responding to a statement or question while gossiping with a friend or neighbour. This opening sets the tone for much of the poem.

Tiresias is initially presented as a middle-aged or elderly man, conventional, set in his ways, happy to wear an old 'patched' tweed jacket and 'his gardening kecks' and take the dog for a walk (6–8). His habit of hearing the 'first cuckoo of spring' (11) and then writing to *The Times* is viewed with contempt by Mrs Tiresias. She has usually heard it first, though she doesn't 'let on' (15). In the Greek myth Tiresias is of similar age. He is the blind prophet or seer, a priest of Zeus, who like the Tiresias of the poem undergoes a sex change. There are several versions of the tale, but the one most suited to Duffy's poem tells that while out walking one day, Tiresias is offended by the sight of two coupling snakes. He takes his stick to them in an attempt to separate them, and in doing so angers Zeus' wife and sister, Hera, the goddess of marriage and childbirth. Her rage at Tiresias' interference with the sexual act spurs her into action and she punishes him by changing his gender. Duffy's Tiresias shares the same prudishness as the Tiresias of the myth. '*Don't kiss me in public,*' he snaps to his wife, '*I don't want folk getting the wrong idea*' (55–7). The Tiresias in his female skin is afraid of being considered a lesbian. In the version of the myth above, one account says that Tiresias kills the female snake, an action which suggests **misogyny**.

CONTEXT

Hera, the queen of heaven, is often portrayed with a pomegranate, the **symbol** of fertility and death. The pomegranate also figures in the myth of Persephone (dealt with by Duffy in 'Demeter').

CONTEXT

In Greek mythology Tiresias, after his change, is sometimes portrayed as a prostitute or courtesan of great accomplishment.

Duffy also subverts the figure of Tiresias the prophet of the myth. In the poem it is Mrs Tiresias and not her husband who experiences a premonition that something strange is afoot in the woods. The 'faint sneer of thunder' (20) she hears is both a portent and a **metaphor** for Hera's contempt and condemnation of Tiresias, and the 'sudden heat' she feels suggests trouble ahead (22). When his female face appears in the mirror, Mrs Tiresias swoons. This appearance of the female face in the mirror is reminiscent of the French psychoanalyst Jacques Lacan and his theory of the mirror stage and ideas of the self (see **Contemporary approaches: Psychoanalytic criticism**). Here Duffy explores both gender and the self divided: Tiresias the man has become Tiresias the woman.

QUESTION What are the differences in Tiresias' character before and after his change? Are there any similarities?

Once Mrs Tiresias has recovered from the shock of seeing her husband changed, she adopts a stoical approach: 'Life has to go on' (33). In sisterly affection she helps Tiresias adapt to his circumstances. It is only when he exhibits the same old character traits – self-centredness, self-pity and prudishness – that she loses patience. His comic inability to deal with menstruation, '*The curse*' (54), without fuss leads to a split. Here Duffy is playing with a **cliché**: the complaint that if men had to deal with periods they would be unable to cope. '*The curse*' has another meaning here too. It refers to Hera's curse and Tiresias' view of his situation that being a woman is a curse. Ultimately he prefers the company of men, as Mrs Tiresias discovers. He also appears on television telling women 'how, as a woman himself, / he knew how we felt' (69–70). **Irony** is, of course, intended here. Tiresias is still a man. Indeed, his relationships with men suggest, in this context, homosexuality. Furthermore, as a woman he shows no sisterly traits; instead he is a flirt. So Mrs Tiresias turns elsewhere for affection.

The final verse marks a shift in mood. Until now it has been informal, the language **colloquial**, and the form of the poem has suited this style. Written in **free verse**, the verses are punctuated every so often by single lines, set apart: 'It got worse' (58), 'I gritted my teeth' (75) and so on. These have served to reinforce the everyday **register**. But the final verse gives way to **lyricism**. The shift signifies Mrs Tiresias' change of mood, and the opening line tells us why. The focus is on a new lover, who is a woman – ironically the kind of relationship most feared by Tiresias.

The image 'her bite at the fruit of my lips' (87), for example, refers to the female genitals as well as the mouth. When together they meet Tiresias at a ball, Mrs Tiresias observes her twin relationships. There is a clever sleight of hand here. What does she mean when she says: 'and I noticed then his hands, her hands' (92)? Is she referring to the new female lover and Tiresias? Or is she referring to Tiresias alone? Both meanings apply. As well as exploring their separate natures, she locates Tiresias' dual sexuality. This exploration of what identity and gender mean is a common **feminist** theme in women's writing (for further discussion of the notion of transformation in women's writing see **Revisionism**). The final verse is also a love poem to the 'violet eyes' (82) and 'the slow caress' (84) of her new lover. Although Mrs Tiresias is still speaking, we can almost hear the poet's voice in the background. The shift from an informal, humorous style throughout most of the poem to a sensitive, lyrical style in the last verse makes it seem more personal, and we see that the poem has become a celebration of lesbian love.

CONTEXT

Tiresias is asked by Hera and Zeus to resolve an argument between them over who experiences the greatest pleasure in lovemaking: the man or the woman. Tiresias claims that women derive nine parts of the pleasure, and men one. Duffy is no doubt aware of this legend when she refers to Tiresias as sexually prudish in his relationships with powerful men (62–5).

GLOSSARY

6 **kecks** trousers

8 **Harris tweed** a traditional, quality cloth made in Scotland

PILATE'S WIFE

- Pontius Pilate's wife witnesses the entry of Jesus of Nazareth into Jerusalem before his trial.
- Jesus appears to her in a dream and she pleads for his release.

Pontius Pilate's wife, the speaker of the poem, witnesses the entry into Jerusalem of Jesus of Nazareth before his trial and Crucifixion and comes face to face with him. He has a powerful effect on her, and when he appears to her in a dream, she is moved to plead for his release.

CONTEXT

Pontius Pilate was the Roman governor of Judaea from AD26–36. When Christ was condemned to death, he was taken to Pilate to be executed. According to all the Christian gospels, Pilate refused to recognise Christ's guilt, but gave way to the demands of the crowd and permitted his execution.

COMMENTARY

The poet describes the marked shift in emotions felt by the speaker as she witnesses the events leading up to and the aftermath of the

CONTEXT

Pilate's wife is nameless in the New Testament, but other Christian traditions have given her various names: Procula, Procla or Claudia Procula.

CONTEXT

According to the Gospel of Matthew, Procula, Pilate's wife, sent a message to her husband requesting that he distance himself from the execution of Christ: 'Have thou nothing to do with that just man: for I have suffered many things this day in a dream because of him' (27:19). In the Greek Orthodox Church Procula has been canonised and is known as St Procula or Procla.

CONTEXT

In Christian theology the Passion refers to Christ's mental anguish and physical torture from the Last Supper with his disciples to his trial and Crucifixion.

trial of Jesus of Nazareth – or as it is known in Christian theology, Christ's suffering or Passion. Though the events of the trial and the Crucifixion and Pilate's wife's part in it are not fully recreated here, the biblical story forms a **subtext** running through the poem, against which she makes her own judgement of her husband.

Pilate is ineffectual. In the biblical account he is unable to stand by his judgement that Jesus is innocent and instead acts expediently, washing his hands of him literally and **figuratively**, so condemning Jesus to certain death. Hands are a recurring **motif** in the poem. The first words refer to hands. A reference to hands then recurs in the third line, then in the fourth, and again in the final verse. Pilate's hands are effete, lacking in strength, a **metaphor** for his own nature. His 'pale, mothy touch' is insubstantial and makes his wife 'flinch' (4). They are not hands she can love; nor can they arouse her. In contrast the Nazarene has strong, workmanlike 'brown hands' (14). Pilate's are pale and bloodless, lifeless even, 'with pearly nails, like shells' (2). Jesus' hands are flesh and blood, though 'each tough palm' is 'skewered / by a nail' (15–16) and his blood is spilled.

It is also the touch of the Nazarene's hands in the speaker's dream in the fourth verse that transforms her, as though his touch has performed a miracle. This is the man who according to the gospels has a profound effect on all who meet him, and she is drawn to him erotically and passionately. There is a suggestion that she experiences stigmata – wounds that correspond to those of the crucified Jesus – and there are also **connotations** of sexual blood as though it were a sexual awakening or initiation: 'His brown hands touched me. Then it hurt. / Then blood' (14–15). The Passion can therefore be understood to have a **double meaning**, since the poem deals both with the trial and Crucifixion of Christ, and the speaker's passion for the man, Jesus.

In the second verse before she has seen him, the wife's interest is merely voyeuristic. She creeps out with her maid, 'bored stiff' (7), to watch the spectacle of Jesus' entry into Jerusalem before the trial. His animal magnetism is overwhelming: 'I mean he looked at *me*. My God. / His eyes were eyes to die for' (10–11). We cannot mistake the several meanings of 'My God' here. It is an exclamation, and a reference to the biblical God. But it is also the man, the lover, the 'someone else' (5) that Pilate's wife has been longing for. Jesus' humanness rather than his mystical nature concerns the poet. Pilate's wife does not believe he is a spiritual being: 'Was he God? Of course not' (24).

After her transformation she is motivated to plead for his life, but Pilate deliberately looks away from his wife. Just as Jesus is judged at his trial, so Pilate's wife sits in judgement on her husband and his 'useless, perfumed hands' (21). These are guilty hands, and the act of washing them is an attempt by Pilate to rid himself of guilt. In the biblical account Pilate believes Jesus to be innocent of any crime. In the poem this is given added impact, for the last words of the poem tell us that unlike his wife, Pilate believes the Nazarene is indeed God. Like Queen Herod he is witnessing the decline of the old beliefs and the rise of Christianity.

The poem is written in six **quatrains** in **iambic pentameter**. Both are traditional forms, and suit the ancient biblical account. In each quatrain the poet introduces a new idea or development. However, Duffy frequently breaks the **metre** by using both **caesura** and **run-on lines** – for example 'I tripped ... looked up / and there he was. His face? Ugly' (8–9) – so that certain words and thoughts are emphasised and the flow is either interrupted or carried into the next verse. A completely regular metre might suggest that the poem's subject was uncomplicated or that the passage of thoughts was smooth, reflective. In the last line the caesura is heavily used and the words emphatic, and the reader is left wondering what personal conflict might ensue for Pilate if he believes the Nazarene to be God.

GLOSSARY

5 **Nazarene** Jesus of Nazareth

19 **Barabbas** prisoner released in place of Christ

23 **Place of Skulls** Calvary, the hill where Jesus was crucified; the name comes from the Latin *calvaria*, meaning 'skull'

CHECK THE NET

There are numerous depictions of different scenes from the Passion in art. One artist who emphasises Christ's physicality is Michelangelo Merisi da Caravaggio (c.1571–1610); to view his paintings *Christ at the Column*, *Crowning with Thorns* and *The Entombment*, visit **www.wga.hu**, find Caravaggio under 'C' and look at the years 1603–7.

CONTEXT

The Greek storyteller Aesop was a slave around the sixth century BC. His fables were first assembled in a volume as *Aesopica.* Historical information is, however, unreliable. Much later in 1484 the fables were printed in England by William Caxton as *The History and Fables of Aesop.*

Mrs Aesop

- Mrs Aesop is tired of her husband, his moralising and his fables, and details the source of her annoyance and boredom.
- She takes revenge by creating her own fable at his expense.

Mrs Aesop, the wife of the ancient Greek storyteller, has endured Aesop and his fables for many years. She draws on his fables to describe her discontent and finally uses them to emasculate him.

Commentary

The poem opens with a curt blasphemy, and tells us that Aesop could 'bore for Purgatory', then follows with a sharp delivery that brings to mind a **rap**, both in rhythm and rhyme: 'He was small, / didn't prepossess. So he tried to impress' (1–2). Mrs Aesop's damning statement sets the tone for the rest of the poem. She shows little mercy for her husband, who was, according to some historical records, unprepossessing and small in stature.

Aesop's fables are pivotal to the poem. They are continually **alluded** to, turned on their head and used in wordplay, and all at Aesop's expense – see Duffy's crudely **satirical** take on the 'bird in the hand' proverb (3–5).

CONTEXT

The tortoise and the hare is one of the most famous of Aesop's fables. A hare ridicules a tortoise for his slow speed and the tortoise challenges the hare to a race. The hare, confident he can win, takes a nap, while the tortoise, slow but sure, passes him and wins. Aesop's moral is that slow and steady wins the race.

The fable of the hare and tortoise is also evoked to humorous effect. Aesop draws his wife's attention to the moral of the tale, while the two animal **protagonists**, ignorant of their fame, quietly go about their business, the 'tortoise, somebody's pet, / creeping, slow as marriage, up the road' (13–14), the **simile** underlining Mrs Aesop's discontent with her marriage.

Duffy draws on **colloquialism** as well as abusive language and proverbs, and the poem is constructed in **free verse**, all within five **quintains**. Occasionally rhyme is used, and other devices such as repetition (for example 'What', 16–17) and **alliteration** ('look, then leap', 6), **caesura** (5, 15) and **run-on lines** (20–1), common in most of the poems in the collection. Here they help to vary the pace and give Mrs Aesop's voice the necessary qualities of exasperation, irritation and anger as she stops, complains or remonstrates.

At one time Aesop's fables were considered edifying, and would have been the mainstay of a child's moral education. Today the original fables are unfashionable, and to the modern reader their tone seems archaic and self-righteous rather than wise. Mrs Aesop would concur. She reports her husband's words from time to time, only to abuse him (14–15). Her voice is often strident and the reader might feel pity for Aesop, if his wife's delivery was not so comical and he not so patronising. He is presented as an unattractive figure, 'Tedious' (5) and ponderous, in thrall to his famous stories and their messages. They give him status and respect, though not from his wife.

It is not only Aesop's homilies that bore his wife. Mrs Aesop has an even greater complaint, hinted at earlier in the simile 'slow as marriage' (14). When he tells her that '*Action, Mrs A., speaks louder / than words*' (19–20), it touches a raw nerve. Not only must she endure his moralising, but also his lack of sexual prowess. Sex, she complains, 'was diabolical' (21); worse, it seems, than the fables. This is the real source of her grievance. In a fit of anger she creates a cruel fable for Aesop 'about a little cock that wouldn't crow' (22), a **metaphor** for impotency, and threatens in **Grand Guignol** fashion to take an axe and cut off his '*tail*' or penis (24). This is the ultimate threat to his masculinity and finally silences Aesop. It also changes the power relations between husband and wife, so that Mrs Aesop gains the upper hand. In one final gesture she demonstrates her superiority by taking the proverb 'He who laughs last, laughs longest' and demonstrating in the last line that *she* will laugh 'last, longest' (25).

GLOSSARY

1 **Purgatory** in Christianity, mainly Catholicism, the place in which souls suffer for their earthly sins before being accepted into heaven

21 **fable** a short story, often with animal characters, that provides a moral

CHECK THE BOOK

If you wish to read any of the fables, Aesop's *The Complete Fables* (1998), translated by Olivia and Robert Temple, is a good edition.

CHECK THE FILM

Aesop's Film Fables is a series of animated short films of Aesop's fables, made by American cartoonist Paul Terry. The series began in 1921, and finally came to an end in 1933.

CHECK THE NET

It is possible to read Aesop's fables online. Go to **www.aesopfables.com**

MRS DARWIN

- Mrs Darwin on a visit to the zoo with her husband makes an important observation.

The poem is laid out in the form of a diary, mimicking Charles Darwin's notes, which were careful records of his observations of animal and plant species.

COMMENTARY

This four-liner is a joke. It **satirises** the eminent Victorian naturalist Charles Darwin and depends for its effect on some understanding of his theories. His principal theory that species evolved through natural selection caused a furore in Victorian society. The implication was that humans had evolved from animals, namely apes. This contradicted the accepted belief, set down in the Book of Genesis, that God had made the world in seven days; and it ushered in the sceptical modern age.

Duffy takes Darwin's theory and gives it to Mrs Darwin. In the poem it is she who makes the imaginative leap to identify the relationship between humans and apes – and all at Darwin's expense, since the poem is an insult as well as a joke. The **insult poem**, though personal, is not to be taken seriously. It is a tease and often includes **hyperbole**. In this case the last line is stretched to accentuate the punch line. The 'oo' rhyme, which occurs in the first, second and fourth lines ('*1852*', 'Zoo' and 'you'), adds humour both because the sound lends itself to comedy and because it occurs so frequently. 'Mrs Darwin' is also a **performance poem** or comic turn, and Duffy has often included it in performance along with 'Mrs Icarus', the other insult poem in *The World's Wife*.

CONTEXT

Darwin (1809–82) describes how offspring vary slightly from their parents. Those traits that make the offspring better adapted to their environment will be encouraged by the process of natural selection; this in turn leads to the evolution of new species. Darwin's theory is fundamental to modern biological sciences. His most notable works are *The Origin of Species by Means of Natural Selection* (1859) and *The Descent of Man and Selection in Relation to Sex* (1871).

WWW. CHECK THE NET

Caricatures of Darwin as an ape were common in the nineteenth century, after his publications. To view some of these, together with some more serious portraits of the man himself, go to **http://commons.wikimedia.org** and search for Charles Darwin.

MRS SISYPHUS

- Mrs Sisyphus observes her husband at work. He is pushing a stone up a hill for eternity, which he does with obsessive commitment.
- He ignores his wife's angry protestations and she contemplates her future.

Mrs Sisyphus is infuriated at her husband's obsessive attention to his work, which is endlessly pushing a stone up a hill. She viciously mocks his foolishness but, unable to deter him from the pointless task, she reflects on the futility of her circumstances and those of other women.

COMMENTARY

Duffy's 'Mrs Sisyphus' owes as much to Albert Camus' essay *Le Mythe de Sisyphe* (*The Myth of Sisyphus*) as it does to the original myth. For Camus, Sisyphus has no meaning to his life; he is condemned to the daily grind of pushing the stone up the hill. This daily grind can be seen as **symbolic**. In the modern world, Camus says, our lives, particularly our working lives, are pointless, and consist of nothing more than repetitive and meaningless tasks. To think otherwise is delusional. Mrs Sisyphus recognises this absurdity and the poem is a **satire** on modern life. Her complaint is a common female one: that men's lives are dominated by work, the drive to succeed and the status it confers. 'Think of the perks', says Sisyphus (6), who has achieved some fame as an endearing eccentric: 'Folk flock from miles around just to gawk' (11). But for Mrs Sisyphus, her husband's endeavours are blatant stupidity.

Feminists would say that the stereotypical role for women has always been primarily domestic, while men's identity is tied to their position and power in the wider world. Duffy suggests in this poem that not a great deal has changed by the late twentieth century and these roles still remain. But she also suggests that women have recognised the absurdity of the male work ethic and do not especially want to pursue it: 'What use is a perk, I shriek, / when you haven't the time to pop open a cork' (7–8) – when there is no time to enjoy life.

The poem draws on insult, and is told in an offhand abusive manner conveying the depth of Mrs Sisyphus' anger and discontent. The first verse opens with a **quintain** that has a jolting rhythm and heavy downward **end rhyme**. It is so heavily accented that it is close to **doggerel**, and the poet is clearly calling on this to create a comic effect. The rhythm also encourages the reader to experience Sisyphus' fruitless task itself: we can feel the poem

CONTEXT

In Greek mythology the avaricious Sisyphus, king of Corinth, is punished for his misdeeds by Hades, god of the underworld. His punishment – to roll the stone to the top of the hill, only to have it roll down again – is for eternity. Hence a 'Sisyphean task' or a 'labour of Sisyphus' means an endless, fruitless job.

CONTEXT

Camus (1913–60) was a French dramatist, novelist and essayist. In his essay *Le Mythe de Sisyphe* Sisyphus is the hero of the absurd, the man who from time to time becomes aware of the illogicality and meaningless of life. Although he denied the connection, Camus is often linked to **existentialism**, whose main proponents were Jean-Paul Sartre (1905–80), Martin Heidegger (1889–1976) and Simone de Beauvoir (1908–86).

CHECK THE BOOK

Clarke in his poem 'Burnley' creates a similar comic effect to the first verse of 'Mrs Sisyphus'. 'Burnley' can be found in *The POP! Anthology: The Poetry Olympics Party Anthology,* edited by Michael Horowitz (2000).

CONTEXT

Noah is an Old Testament figure found in Genesis (Chapters 5–10). God, discontent with humanity, warned Noah that he would send the Flood to destroy the world. The Lord told Noah to build an ark that would float on the water; in this he was to take with him a male and female of every species.

CONTEXT

Johann Sebastian Bach (1685–1750) was an extremely prolific German composer.

metaphorically pushing the stone up the hill. It begs to be read out loud. It is a **performance poem** as well as a **satire**, and reminiscent of the poetry of John Cooper Clarke (b.1949), who uses similar rhythms and rhyme for comic effect.

Rhyme continues throughout, and though in the second part it becomes **free verse** and the lines vary in length, the lumpy rhythm is maintained, helped by the rhyme. It is only in the final part of the poem that a different mood creeps in. Mrs Sisyphus bemoans her lot. She is lonely, and compares herself to those other unsung wives whose famous husbands – the biblical Noah and the composer Bach – also showed unremitting dedication to their work, to the detriment of their marriages. The foolishness of her husband's life impinges on her, and since she seems powerless to prevent it she achieves a kind of tragic stature within this dark comic absurdity. Having been vociferous in her condemnation of her husband, her voice is 'reduced' by the end of the poem 'to a squawk' (29), her smile 'to a twisted smirk' (30). As she contemplates the 'deepening murk of the hill' (31), the future looks bleak as well as absurd.

GLOSSARY

2	**kirk** Scottish for church
5	**dirk** dagger worn by Scottish highlanders
10	**dork** fool
11	**gawk** stare
13	**lark** prank

MRS FAUST

- Mrs Faust recalls the history of her life with Faust, who sold his soul to Mephistopheles.
- The marriage disintegrates and she begins to lead her own life.
- When Faust is finally damned we discover that he had never had a soul to sell.

Faust's life, told through his wife, is one of avarice and deception, and it becomes increasingly corrupt after he sells his soul to Mephistopheles, the devil. For a while, Mrs Faust goes her own separate way. When the devil finally arrives to claim his dues, Mrs Faust reveals to the reader her husband's ultimate deceit: he had no soul to sell.

COMMENTARY

In the poem Faust and his wife are first cast as aggressive social climbers, set in a hard-nosed modern capitalist world. Status, individual achievement and the acquisition of material goods are the values by which they live. Duffy wittily depicts them following pursuits not untypical of many middle-class couples. Scholarly achievement, in keeping with the Faust legend, is desirable as a means to an end: 'BA. MA. Ph.D.' (8); and increasingly they acquire the affectations of their position – 'Two towelled bathrobes. Hers. His' (9) – leading to more impressive material possessions: 'Fast cars. A boat with sails. / A second home in Wales' (12–13). The poem rushes along in **free verse** like the Fausts' fast living. Years are described in a few words helped by repetition and rhyme: 'shacked up, split up, / made up, hitched up' (4–5).

Life for Mrs Faust, however, starts to sour when she realises that her husband is wedded to the life and not to her (21–2). He becomes a hedonist, seeking thrills and continual gratification. For Faust power is tied to wealth, and the drive for power is overwhelming. As he acquires more wealth, so he becomes more avaricious and takes greater risks, until he seeks the final transgression: a pact with the devil. Mrs Faust returns home one night to the smell of cigar smoke, 'hellish, oddly sexy' (43), coming from Faust's study, and she hears a strange guest laughing. The cigar is phallic, a **symbol** of male power. The guest is the devil. Faust now has unlimited earthly power captured in the carnal image 'the world, / as Faust said, / spread its legs' (46–8), which also suggests Faust's contempt for women. Everything is obscenely available to him. He becomes a politician, is knighted, becomes a lord, even 'Cardinal, Pope', and 'knew more than God' (56–7), and reaches the dizzy heights of walking 'on the moon' (61). He is thoroughly corrupt, investing in arms deals and 'smart bombs' (65). His end can only be moral destruction.

CONTEXT

In the legend, Faust sells his soul to the devil in return for twenty-four years of unlimited pleasure, knowledge and power. This legend has inspired many writers. *The Tragical History of Dr Faustus*, written by Christopher Marlowe (1564–93), was published in 1604 and follows the structure of a medieval morality play, dealing with human temptation, sin, salvation and death. Since Marlowe's play, there have been other notable interpretations of the Faust story, including Johann Wolfgang von Goethe's plays *Faust Part I* (1808) and *Faust Part II* (1832), and Thomas Mann's novel *Doktor Faustus* (1948).

CONTEXT

With the line 'spun gold from hay' (76) Duffy is referring to the fairy tale 'Rumpelstiltskin', included in the 1812 collection by the Brothers Grimm, in which the miller's daughter must spin hay into gold. The poet uses this as a **metaphor** for Mrs Faust's money-making ventures.

CONTEXT

Faust boasts to his wife that he *'spent the night being pleasured / by a virtual Helen of Troy'* (92–3). Helen of Troy was renowned for her outstanding beauty; in Greek literary tradition, beginning with Homer, she is married to King Menelaus and abducted by Paris, so bringing about the Trojan War. In Marlowe's play *Dr Faustus* she is 'the face that launched a thousand ships'.

Mrs Faust, meanwhile, crazily pursues her own attempts at transformation through travel, cosmetic surgery and alternative lifestyles until, at the age of forty, dissatisfied, 'berserk' and desperate (87–8), she breaks and returns home. There she finds Faust and reports his story through his words. He has reached the end of the road. The only new experience will be with the devil, Mephistopheles, who will be arriving shortly to claim the debt. At which point the devil, like a pantomime villain, emerges on cue, 'right through the terracotta Tuscan tiles' (114), and drags Faust down to hell. The Faust legend in Duffy's hands has become a comedy. And Faust has the last **ironic** laugh too, as the punchline reveals: Mephistopheles cannot claim Faust's soul because he never had one to sell – a fact intimated earlier, as Faust, 'oddly smirking' (116), disappeared into the fiery furnace.

And what of Mrs Faust? Is she so very different from her husband? Her numerous and erratic forays into spiritual enlightenment are merely superficial. She inherits his wealth, and casually comments, 'C'est la vie' (127). Certainly she becomes ill, but physically, not spiritually or morally. She buys a new kidney, not a new heart. And her final comment on Faust as 'clever, cunning [and] callous' (134) suggests a sneaking admiration for him.

The poem can be read as a witty critique on the world we live in. The Faustian legend and its moral struggle has lost its impact if our values are merely acquisitive ones and our sense of self-worth derived only from the power that wealth brings. Duffy seems to be asking: has capitalism brought us to the point where everything can be bought and sold and everyone has a price?

GLOSSARY

21	**kudos** renown, glory
26	**t'ai chi** Chinese system of slow-moving exercises
27	**Feng Shui** Chinese practice of arranging space and objects in order to achieve harmony with the environment
	colonic irrigation cleaning the intestines with water
33	**Soho** London district famous for its clubs and sex shops
50	**Right Hon.** Right Honourable
	KG Knight of the Order of the Garter

GLOSSARY

63 **Havana** Cuban cigar

72 **Bo-Peep** female shepherd from a nursery rhyme; also slang for someone who has lost their senses, as in 'Little Bo Peep has lost her sheep'

CONTEXT

A possible contender for the 'real' Faust is Dr Johann Georg Faustus (*c.*1480–*c.*1540), a German astrologer and alchemist who was alleged to have practised necromancy. Various legends grew up around him.

DELILAH

- Delilah tells how her warrior lover wants to become tender and loving.
- When he falls asleep she cuts off his hair, the source of his strength.

In this poem, Delilah informs us that her warrior lover wishes to learn tenderness. He describes his prowess, and his strong masculine physique and nature are depicted, together with his desire for change. So when he falls asleep Delilah cuts off his hair, and with it his masculine strength.

COMMENTARY

Duffy rewrites the biblical tale of Samson and Delilah. To **feminists**, Delilah has become a **misogynistic symbol** of the femme fatale or treacherous woman who is a man's undoing because of her betrayal of Samson in the Bible. Asked by his enemies to discover the secret of his superhuman strength, Delilah uses her sexual powers to beguile Samson and discovers that the source of his power is his hair. Duffy takes the biblical tale, reworks it and places it in a modern setting.

CHECK THE BOOK

The biblical story of Samson and Delilah can be found in the Old Testament in the Book of Judges (16:4–20).

The poem is an intimate scene between two latter-day lovers. The male lover, softened by Delilah's presence, confides in her as he takes a swig from his beer. It could be the opening scene from a Hollywood film. The soldier hero confesses how his masculine prowess, his fearlessness, shuts down his gentle side, and he guides Delilah's fingers 'over the scar / over his heart' (16–17), over his damaged emotions. He wants to get in touch with the feminine. An image of a New Man emerges, a term coined in the 1990s to

CHECK THE NET

There have been many depictions in art of Samson and Delilah. To view some paintings of this biblical story by artists such as Sir Anthony Van Dyck (1599–1641) and Sir Peter Paul Rubens (1577–1640), visit **www.biblical-art.com** and search for Samson and Delilah.

CHECK THE FILM

Samson and Delilah (1996), directed by Nicolas Roeg and starring Elizabeth Hurley as Delilah, was adapted from the biblical tale. Samson, played by Eric Thal, is depicted as showing little emotional vulnerability.

describe a man in touch with his feelings and aware of women's issues. The male lover declares, as if lamenting his condition, that he 'cannot be gentle, or loving, or tender'; instead he has 'to be strong' (19–20): a victim of what **feminism** describes as the **phallocentric** society. He asks Delilah, 'What is the cure?' (21). Once their lovemaking is over and his voice is soft and low, she convinces herself that 'he wanted to change' (30). So she takes him at his word. She cuts off his hair, the **symbol** of his manly strength, in order that he may be renewed.

We can read this poem in more than one way. We might, for example, view Delilah's act as one that is sympathetic to her lover's desire to learn tenderness, and that in following his wishes she is his support. This also reverses the traditional image of Delilah as the femme fatale. But we could also ask whether the poet is serious. Is the male lover's desire for tenderness merely pillow talk, the intimate exchange between two people which often evaporates outside the bedroom? Is Delilah's conviction that her lover wants to change tongue-in-cheek? We could argue that Duffy is playing with the popular notion that most women want a level of intimacy that men apparently find difficult but play along with for their own ends.

In support of this reading is the depiction of the male lover, which is similar to that of Superman – not to be taken entirely seriously – and the old adage 'All brawn and no brain' seems appropriate as he recounts his death-defying feats in the second verse. We might even think, in this modern setting, that to 'rip out the roar / from the throat of a tiger, / or gargle with fire' (7–9) might be a touch exaggerated. Another comic spectacle is the image of his gigantic body, fallen and vulnerable on the floor, snoring (33–6), an incongruous image for such a man. Delilah is sharper than him and quite prepared to resort to devious behaviour: 'I nibbled the purse of his ear' (4) is an **allusion** to Delilah's payment in the biblical tale for betraying Samson, and here perhaps a **metaphor** for Delilah's revenge. In testing his claim to be afraid of nothing, even intimacy, Delilah seems to get revenge against the story as well as her lover. Is she casting a backward glance in contempt at the old tale when she sharpens her scissors and snips gleefully 'at the black and biblical air' (38), before purposely and ardently relieving her lover of 'every lock of his hair' (42)?

GLOSSARY

10 **Minotaur** in Greek mythology a creature part man, part bull, killed by Theseus

ANNE HATHAWAY

- Anne Hathaway, the wife of William Shakespeare, recalls the bed she shared with her husband.
- Shakespeare's imagination becomes part of her own thoughts, and he lives on in her memory.

Shakespeare's widow, Anne Hathaway, celebrates the love she shared with her husband. His creative world becomes part of the remembered intimacy between the two lovers, so that Shakespeare still exists for his wife, through her memory and imagination.

COMMENTARY

This poem is a celebration of Anne Hathaway's love for her dead husband, spoken through her, and in her own name. She is not given her famous husband's wifely title, unlike most of the wives in the collection. This immediately empowers her and suggests an equal partnership. The poem is written in the form of a traditional love poem, a **Shakespearean sonnet**.

There are not many love poems in *The World's Wife*. Aside from 'Demeter', which celebrates love between mother and daughter, and possibly 'Queen Kong', though that is more **satire** than love poem, 'Anne Hathaway' is the only poem that truly celebrates heterosexual love. This is a mark of the poet's respect for Shakespeare; the **sonnet** is a tribute to his work. He himself was a prolific writer of sonnets – another reason why the form is an ideal one for Duffy to choose (for further discussion of the sonnet see **Poetic forms: The sonnet**).

CONTEXT

Little is known about Anne Hathaway (*c.*1556–1623). It is thought she was born and brought up in Shottery, near Stratford-upon-Avon. Her assumed family home is now a museum. She married Shakespeare in 1582, and had three children with him: Susanna, the eldest; and twins, Judith and Hamnet.

CHECK THE BOOK

The full quote from Shakespeare's will states: 'Item I gyve unto my wief my second best bed with the furniture.' Lucy Gent in *Albion's Classicism: Visual Arts in England, 1550–1660* (1995) points out that the marriage bed represented not only fidelity but identity, and would have been the most important possession in the household.

CHECK THE BOOK

Shakespeare: A Life (1998) by Park Honan, and *Shakespeare: The Biography* (2005) by Peter Ackroyd give excellent studies of Anne Hathaway and her relationship with Shakespeare.

The quotation at the beginning of the poem is an **epigraph** from Shakespeare's will, in which he leaves his wife the second best bed. This has proved a curiosity down the years, and scholars have puzzled over its meaning. Duffy takes the view, as many do, that the custom at the time was to reserve the best bed for guests (11). In the poem the second best bed therefore becomes the central **metaphor** for marital love. It is the place where Anne Hathaway's intimate thoughts and past experiences are tied to Shakespeare's creativity and played out in her imagination. The 'spinning world' of the first line that she inhabits in her mind is the world of Shakespeare in all its abundance. The landscapes in the second line are those of the Forest of Arden in *A Midsummer Night's Dream* and *As You Like It*; the battlements of Elsinore in *Hamlet*; and the seas of *The Tempest*, where 'he would dive for pearls' (3): a metaphor for lovemaking and also an acknowledgement of Ariel's song 'Full fathom five' (*The Tempest*, I.2.399–405). Shakespeare's techniques are reflected in images of love: 'his touch / a verb dancing in the centre of a noun' (6–7). His inventive use of language meant that he created words when there were none suitable, and turned grammar on its head. In *The Merry Wives of Windsor*, the Welsh parson Sir Hugh Evans turns a noun into a verb, announcing, 'I will description the matter to you' (I.1.195–6).

Duffy gives Anne Hathaway an articulate and **lyrical** voice like her husband's as she joyously recalls their lovemaking. Hers is a 'softer rhyme / to his' (5–6), a **feminine rhyme**, as though Duffy is referring to both Anne Hathaway's feminine poetic voice and, less directly, her own. The rhyme is also a metaphor for the wife and husband's unity. In much the same way, other poetic and linguistic devices are referred to and used in the poem to represent this marriage of love and language, and in so doing the poet draws attention to the poetic act. The words 'on', 'body', 'softer' and 'assonance' (5–6) are all examples of **assonance**. The poem is full of traditional poetic techniques. The **consonance** of 'My living laughing love' (12) conveys the exuberance of Anne Hathaway's memories, while **alliteration** and **anaphora** – 'by touch, by scent, by taste' (10) – accentuate their pleasure. Anne Hathaway even dreams that her husband has written her, created her as a character. The bed is the page but also the theatre of their own sensual drama:

> Some nights, I dreamed he'd written me, the bed
> a page beneath his writer's hands. Romance
> and drama played by touch, by scent, by taste. (8–10)

We could even argue that Anne Hathaway is presented here as a **construct** of Shakespeare's imagination. Duffy's strong visual image resonates as other guests sleep in the best bed, their prose merely 'dribbling' (12), lacking the creative impetus of Shakespeare's verse.

The final **rhyming couplet** brings us back to the overarching metaphor of the second best bed and to the summing up, the couplet's purpose. As final lines they not only bring the poem to a conclusion but also serve as an acknowledgement of her lover's death. Anne Hathaway refers to his living presence 'in the casket of my widow's head' (13). A casket is both a strongbox where the most valuable possessions are kept and a coffin. Here then lies Shakespeare, immortal in his wife's imagination and through his own creative genius, celebrated in a poem by Carol Ann Duffy.

CHECK THE FILM

The Pillow Book (1996), directed by Peter Greenaway and starring Vivian Wu and Ewan McGregor, explores the relationship between sex, pleasure and language. In it two lovers write on each other's bodies.

QUEEN KONG

- Queen Kong, a giant gorilla, falls in love with a man who comes to her island.
- After he has left she decides to follow him to New York, where they live together for many years.
- When he dies Queen Kong preserves him and hangs him around her neck so he will always be with her.

Queen Kong, the female counterpart of the giant gorilla King Kong, falls in love with a documentary film-maker who has come to her island to study a species of toad. She lavishes her attention on him and, distraught when he returns home, pursues him to New York. After twelve years together he dies, and in memory she preserves him and hangs him around her neck as though he were a piece of jewellery.

CONTEXT

In the 1933 film *King Kong*, a film crew makes a trip to Skull Island, where the leading lady is kidnapped by the giant gorilla Kong. After many attempts she is found, and Kong is captured and taken back to New York to be exhibited. He breaks free, and climbs with Ann to the top of the Empire State Building, where he eventually plunges to his death.

QUESTION Is there any evidence in the poem that Queen Kong's 'man' returns her love?

COMMENTARY

In this poem Duffy takes the characters of King Kong and the fragile, passive heroine, Ann, the gorilla's fixation, from the 1933 film *King Kong*, and neatly brings about a role reversal, so that King Kong becomes female and the love interest is a vulnerable man. Told in a confessional style through the language of popular media – 'All right, he was small, but perfectly formed / and *gorgeous*' (17–18) – Queen Kong is looking back at events in the manner of a flashback from a film. The effect is both comic and touching. In this last respect the poet retains something of the original film, in which the audience feels sympathy for the lovesick beast as we feel sympathy for Queen Kong in her naive assumption that her love is requited. Indeed, we could argue that she is presented here as a lonely woman desperate for love, her size a **metaphor** for how much love she has to give.

Unlike King Kong, however, Queen Kong is no sacrifice. Nor is heterosexual love for her a snare, as it is in many poems in *The World's Wife*. Indeed, she glories in it. It is, however, a snare for the documentary film-maker, who packs his case as quick as he can, 'miming the flight back home / to New York' (31–2) in an attempt to communicate with Queen Kong, when the prize-winning film is complete. Apart from this one act of defiance, where she allows him to leave, he is ineffectual. The events of their love are told entirely from the perspective of Queen Kong, and with considerable bias. She details their bond with conviction, but his words are never reported. She holds all the power and **objectifies** him, treating him like a doll, much as King Kong treats the heroine in the 1933 film, albeit without intentional harm. 'My little man' (2) she calls him, or manikin we might think – a metaphor for the way women such as models can be regarded in a **patriarchal** world.

Unable to come to terms with her loss, she goes on a 'binge for a fortnight' (37), forsakes her island and travels to New York to find him. There follows an absurd image of a 'discreet' Queen Kong as she prowls the streets in search of him (46–7), another indication that she is not an entirely reliable **narrator**. When she finds him she sees a photo of herself above his bed and mistakenly believes it is a manifestation of his love for her. As a prize-winning documentary film-maker, Queen Kong's man would display pictures of his best work. There is also a **subtext** here. The image recalls the poster of the 1933 film, which has long since entered the popular imagination.

After buying her lover presents – not unlike a powerful man buying presents for his mistress – she claims ownership and takes him, dangling 'in the air between my finger / and my thumb in a teasing, lover's way' (59–60), to the top of the Empire State Building. This is the site of the **denouement** in the film, where King Kong plunges to his death. In the poem the lovers apparently spend twelve happy years together, and though there seems to be some mutual affection between them, he nonetheless plays 'his plaintive, lost tunes' (70), an image that reveals his resignation and suggests that it is a less than happy experience for him. The image of the man's tiny 'preserved' body is also darkly comic (75): Duffy, by turning the love interest into jewellery, is wittily calling attention to the way in which women in some circles, such as Hollywood, are still viewed as decorative objects.

The King Kong story has close links with the fairy tale 'Beauty and the Beast', and also with Mary Shelley's *Frankenstein* (1818). In both these stories the creatures are outside humanity and yet have human emotions. Love is the instrument that can break the spell and restore the beast to humanity, though only the fairy story has this outcome. This is also true of Queen Kong, in so far as love is the healer: 'I'd been so *lonely*', she says petulantly (15). There is one essential difference, however. Queen Kong has no desire to become human. She may be a comic figure, but she is perfectly happy in her skin, a powerful and independent female. She is also an eternal optimist and lives in blissful ignorance, believing her love to be requited. She takes comfort that hanging from her neck, against her 'massive, breathing lungs', her erstwhile lover 'in his silent death' sometimes can hear her 'roar' – and is no doubt deafened by it (76–7).

CHECK THE FILM

King Kong (1933) was directed by Merian C. Cooper and starred Fay Wray, Bruce Cabot and Robert Armstrong. Notable remakes include *King Kong: The Legend Reborn* (1976), directed by John Guillermin and starring Jessica Lange, Jeff Bridges and Charles Grodin; and *King Kong* (2005), directed by Peter Jackson and starring Naomi Watts, Jack Black and Andy Serkis.

CHECK THE BOOK

There are two **feminist** rewritings of 'Beauty and the Beast' in *The Bloody Chamber and Other Stories* (1979) by Angela Carter: 'The Courtship of Mr Lyon' and 'The Tiger's Bride'. The latter in particular is an excellent example of **revisionism**. It is useful to compare their treatment with 'Queen Kong'.

GLOSSARY

5	**the Village** Greenwich Village, a formerly bohemian district of New York, now fashionable among wealthy celebrities, though it still has a tolerant attitude to different lifestyles
7	**pastrami on rye** a popular American rye bread sandwich; pastrami is salted spiced beef
56	**Bloomingdale's** famous department store

MEDUSA

- Medusa recounts her story as a jealous wife, doubting her husband's fidelity.
- As the doubt grows she becomes transformed into a monster so that living things that meet her gaze are turned to stone.
- She confronts her husband.

Medusa laments her condition as a wife who doubts her husband's fidelity. She tells how the seed of doubt grows until, consumed with jealousy, she becomes monstrous, with the power to turn all living things to stone. She looks at her image in the mirror and despairs. Her husband returns and she confronts him.

CHECK THE NET

Two compelling images of Medusa are *The Head of Medusa* by Peter Paul Rubens, which can be seen at **www.wga.hu** – search for the title – and *Medusa* by Caravaggio, which you can view at **www.abcgallery.com**

COMMENTARY

Carol Ann Duffy presents us with a very different reason for Medusa's **transformation** into the Gorgon from the one presented in Greek mythology. In the best-known version of the tale Medusa is a nymph whose beauty attracts the sea god Poseidon. When they consummate their relationship in the goddess Athena's sacred temple, Athena in anger transforms Medusa into a Gorgon – a winged female monster with snakes writhing from her head, whose gaze can turn men to stone.

In Duffy's poem we can assume Medusa was once beautiful, since the description of her present state 'now' (8) implies a contrast with her previous appearance: 'My bride's breath soured' (6). In the final lines she is looking back: 'Wasn't I beautiful?' (40). Her inward obsession with what seems at first to be an unnamed jealousy has transformed her outward appearance, so that her hair turns to snakes 'as though my thoughts / hissed and spat on my scalp' (4–5). She is not only transformed into a Gorgon, but she becomes putrid, rotten, with 'bullet tears' (10) and the power to destroy. All things from 'a buzzing bee' (18) to 'a singing bird' (21) to 'a snuffling pig' (27) become lifeless, petrified by her gaze, and a dragon is transformed into a destructive volcano.

'Are you terrified?' Medusa asks at the end of the second verse. A useful comparison might be made here with Sylvia Plath's 'Lady Lazarus', a poem about suicide that includes the disintegration of the body and the self. 'Lady Lazarus' is a companion piece to 'Daddy', written in the early 1960s. Both poems also explore the controlling masculine force that dominates and subjugates female self-expression, and in 'Daddy' the female conflict between this and the desire for masculine love and affirmation is also addressed. In both poems the speaker **metaphorically** kills the masculine. Duffy could be said to explore all these concerns. Medusa's body decays. She is also trapped by her love for her husband, the 'Greek God' (14) and the **symbol** of the conquering hero who it seems here is impervious to her and perhaps to all women: in place of his heart there is a shield, a protection against love. Medusa has also grown old: 'Wasn't I fragrant and young?' (41). Her decay is part of ageing, and her jealousy may not be unfounded. Love has 'gone bad' (31), and her husband seems to dally with 'girls' in order to consort with beauty and youth.

At the end of Plath's poems the female power is reasserted. In 'Lady Lazarus' the speaker rises again and 'eat[s] men like air'. In 'Daddy' a stake is driven into the 'fat black heart'. In 'Medusa', however, the outcome is less certain. She may punish her Greek god in the last line and render him powerless, enticing him – and the reader – to be turned to stone, but the cry 'Look at me now' is a **juxtaposition**. It invites him and us to pity her loss of youth and beauty too. In the Greek myth Medusa is also the victim. The hero Perseus tricks her; he avoids her deadly gaze by seeing her reflection in the mirror of his polished shield, and then beheads her.

CHECK THE BOOK

'Lady Lazarus' and 'Daddy' can be found in Sylvia Plath's *Collected Poems*, published in 1981 with an introduction by Ted Hughes.

CONTEXT

Sylvia Plath (1932–63), a highly regarded American poet, was once married to the British poet Ted Hughes (1930–98). Her poetry collections *Ariel* (1965), *Crossing the Water* (1971) and *Winter Trees* (1972) were all published posthumously.

Circe

- Circe addresses the reader, describing the range of pigs and their features.
- She introduces recipes for pig and the process of preparation and cooking.
- Her thoughts turn to her youth, recalling how she watched the sailors coming ashore in their ships.
- She returns to basting the pig.

CONTEXT

Circe is similar to the witch of European folklore, who possessed magical powers. She was either feared because of her knowledge, which gave her power, or regarded with respect as the wise woman whose knowledge could heal.

Circe addresses the reader directly, calling to mind a celebrity chef preparing food. Her liking for pig is evident as she savours the varied features of different pigs, **personifying** them. As her thoughts turn to her youth and how she watched the sailors coming ashore in their tall ships, she recalls how she once liked men. Finally she returns to basting the pig cooking on a spit.

Commentary

Circe's reference to a vast assortment of pigs can be taken as an **allusion** to the range and variety of men she has encountered, or who exist in the world generally. Their natures, their physical appearance, their manners, are all piglike. **Puns** are used to describe them. We can read the 'boar' as the boring man, and the 'swine' as both pig and contemptible male (2). Choosing the animal itself as a **metaphor** is indicative of her feelings, since 'pig' is also an abusive term, male chauvinist pig being the most obvious. There are sexual **connotations** in their 'oinks', 'grunts' and 'squeals' (6–7) and eroticism in the consumption of pig as food – and this is Circe's real revenge against men. She will eat them and relish the juicy meal in the process.

CONTEXT

Thetis is also a nereid. Compare 'Circe' with 'Thetis', also in *The World's Wife*, and note the characters' different magical powers.

The poem is **satirical** but an understanding of who Circe is and her relationship with Odysseus is necessary to appreciate fully the allusions and satire in the poem. In Greek mythology Circe is depicted as sometimes a nereid but also a sorcerer who uses her knowledge of herbs and magical potions to change into animals any who should cross her. In Homer's *Odyssey* she prepares a feast for

Odysseus and his crew. But the feast is a trap and contains one of Circe's potions, causing the sailors to be **transformed** into pigs. Odysseus, however, is warned and escapes their fate. Circe falls in love with him and subsequently helps him return home. It is only in this last matter that the Circe of the poem differs from that of the myth. She is not the benign Circe who offers a helping hand to her sojourning lover. Rather, men have disappointed her, perhaps because like Odysseus they do not stay. So she decides to undertake a little revenge.

Food can be a replacement for sex or an accompaniment to lust. Certainly Circe enjoys pig, and we can take this to mean both as food and sex. In the second verse she describes the uses of the tongue as the process of oral sex. The language, like the cooking, is succulent and rich. There is heavy **alliteration**, which also adds a note of humour: 'Remember the skills of the tongue – / to lick, to lap, to loosen, lubricate, to lie / in the soft pouch of the face' (15–17). There is an added sting in the **double meaning** of 'lie', for men are duplicitous it seems. All this is comically **juxtaposed** with the practicalities of cooking in which the no-nonsense **imperative** is used: 'Lay two pig's cheeks, with the tongue, / in a dish, and strew it well over with salt' (13–14). One of the most comical and resonant images occurs as she recounts the faces of her past loves. Whether 'handsome' (18) or 'cruel' (20), they all have that telltale sign: 'piggy eyes' (21), those small, ugly, insensitive eyes without depth. This being so, 'Season with mace' (21), Circe abruptly declares, as though throwing spice in her lovers' eyes, like a woman with a mission.

There are other notable techniques used in this poem. Circe as the speaker is **foregrounded** in the poem. Though this is the case in all **dramatic monologues**, here the speaker addresses the readers directly as females, 'nereids and nymphs' (1). The voice is confidential, as though she is sharing a joke with other women at the expense of men. The poem is also self-referential, conscious of its own artifice, when for example drawing attention to the pun 'tongue in cheek' (12).

As the poem progresses, Circe warms to her task. Face and eyes have been dealt with; in the third verse it is the turn of the ear. That ear, she asks **rhetorically**, 'did it listen, ever, to you, to your

CHECK THE NET

The nineteenth-century Pre-Raphaelite painter Edward Burne-Jones (1833–98) depicted Circe in *The Wine of Circe*. John William Waterhouse (1849–1917) painted *Circe Offering the Cup to Odysseus*. To see what features of these paintings correspond with Duffy's poem, visit **www.rossettiarchive.org** and search for 'Wine of Circe'; and **www.wikipedia.org/wiki/Circe** to view Waterhouse's painting.

CHECK THE BOOK

Tanglewood Tales (1853) is a series of Greek myths retold by the American writer Nathaniel Hawthorne (1804–64). The story of Circe is included.

prayers and rhymes' (25)? Of course not, answers the reader. So the recommended treatment for it is to be 'blanched, singed, tossed / in a pot' (22–3), and so on. Every part of the body is examined and cooked until finally the 'hardened' heart is dealt with: 'When the heart of a pig has hardened, dice it small' (30). 'Dice it small' is repeated with emphasis (31). This repetition announces a change of mood, as Circe looks back at her youth. She remembers how she waited romantically for her men at the seashore, for men who came and went, like Odysseus. It is a lyrical and melancholic moment, revealing that Circe as a mythical figure was drawn to love. Youthful hope was not fulfilled, but since it was a long time ago, Circe of the poem does not allow herself to ruminate for long. Instead she turns back to her task with gusto: 'Now, / let us baste that sizzling pig on the spit once again' (38).

GLOSSARY

1	**nereids** water nymphs
	nymphs female spirits of nature in Greek mythology, found on land or in water
21	**mace** a spice from the outer casing of nutmeg

MRS LAZARUS

- Mrs Lazarus tells us how she grieves for her dead husband.
- Time passes and he becomes a memory.
- She meets a schoolteacher and begins her life again, until news comes that Lazarus has risen from the grave.

CHECK THE BOOK

The story of Lazarus can be found in the New Testament in John 11. Lazarus is returned from the dead to his sisters Mary Magdalene and Martha; he leaves the tomb in his shroud.

In the biblical story Jesus raises Lazarus from the dead, restoring him to his grieving sisters. In the poem it is the wife, Mrs Lazarus, who is grieving, and the poem is told through her eyes. As time passes she slowly recovers, so that eventually Lazarus is only a memory. Healed, she meets someone else, a schoolteacher, only to discover that Lazarus has risen from the grave.

COMMENTARY

The poem opens with Mrs Lazarus as the grieving widow. Her pain is acute. She suffers mental anguish in contrast to Lazarus' physical anguish, and the poem is written in heightened, even melodramatic terms: 'I … howled, shrieked, clawed / at the burial stones … retched / his name over and over again, dead, dead' (2–5). The theme of death persists in verses two and three. She tells us how she 'shuffled in a dead man's shoes, / noosed the double knot of a tie' around her own neck (9–10), suggesting that Mrs Lazarus is herself half dead with grief. Though told as a **dramatic monologue**, the poem bears some resemblance to an **elegy**. Written in a regular verse pattern of eight **quintains**, it follows loosely the pattern of the classical elegy: lamentations for the dead person, with eventual acceptance of the loss and finally the process of healing. In 'Mrs Lazarus', however, the twist at the end when Lazarus returns owes more to the **Gothic**.

Gradually she becomes distanced from him through time. Ethereal images of vanishing occur in verses four and five, so that Lazarus is like a disappearing phantom: 'The last hair on his head / floated out from a book' (17–18). Duffy also equates his absence with what she calls 'legend, language' (21), as though he not only belongs to an indistinct past, in the use of the word 'legend', but has also become merely words, divorced from feeling. It is at this point that Mrs Lazarus can begin to live again. The schoolteacher she meets is a strong presence. His arm is flesh and blood and conveys 'the shock / of a man's strength' (22–3) in comparison to the absent Lazarus. Her husband's return is therefore not only unwelcome but is far worse; it is ghoulish: 'I breathed / his stench; my bridegroom in his rotting shroud' (37–8), as though she must remarry a living corpse. This is truly Gothic. Indeed, at times the poem seems set in an unknown past, as folk or Gothic tales are. There is the village blacksmith (33), and Mrs Lazaurus wears 'a shawl of fine air' (27). But there are also modern references: 'black bags' (9) and 'barmaid' (34). In this respect the poem itself seems to hover between two states, the past and the present, as Lazarus hovers between the two states of life and death.

CHECK THE BOOK

Sylvia Plath's 'Lady Lazarus' gives another perspective on the Bible story. It can be found in Plath's *Collected Poems* (1981).

CONTEXT

In the Bible when Jesus first tells Mary that Lazarus will rise from the dead, she takes this to mean the Last Judgement, when according to the Christian religion everyone at the end of time will be allotted to either heaven or hell.

CHECK THE NET

Visit **www.abcgallery.com** to see *The Last Judgement*, a painting by Hieronymus Bosch (1450–1516). Bosch often painted strange creatures, part human. Compare his images with Duffy's depiction of Lazarus in the final verse.

In contemporary **discourse** the name Lazarus has positive **connotations** suggesting rebirth. In the biblical event too, there is great joy at the miracle of Lazarus' resurrection. Here in the poem Lazarus has risen from 'the grave's slack chew' (39), not from the dead. This is a significant distinction and signals a quite different story. Duffy has subverted the meaning of the biblical tale, stripping it of the miraculous, so that Lazarus appears not as one brought back to life but as the undead; some creature in limbo, belonging to neither this world nor any other, 'disinherited, out of his time' (40).

GLOSSARY

12 **Stations of Bereavement** this recalls the Stations of the Cross: in Catholicism each station (there are fourteen) is a picture or carving which represents successive incidents in the passage of Christ from Pilate's house to his Crucifixion at Calvary

PYGMALION'S BRIDE

CONTEXT

Ovid (43BC–c.AD17) was a Roman poet writing in Latin. His *Metamorphoses* is a poem written over fifteen books, approximately two thousand years ago. It tells of the creation and history of the world and contains tales of **transformation** in which a mortal or a god is changed into a plant or animal. Tales of transformation are common in ancient myths.

- Pygmalion has created a statue of a woman, who is the speaker of the poem.
- She describes how Pygmalion brings her to life, but she cannot and does not want to respond to his touch.
- In order to rid herself of him she changes her behaviour, which makes him lose interest.

The sculptor Pygmalion falls in love with a statue he has created. The statue is the speaker of the poem and she describes how she resists his advances, remaining unresponsive. In order to put a stop to his demands she changes her tactics. She becomes warm, responsive and demanding, and successfully frightens him away.

COMMENTARY

In the original Roman tale written by Ovid, Pygmalion, king of Cyprus, carves a female figure from ivory, with whom he falls in love. He prays to the goddess Venus, who takes pity on him and brings the statue to life. A son, Paphos, is born. Duffy twists the Pygmalion myth for her own ends, mainly to address some widely held contemporary views by women about heterosexual relationships. The poet also explores a theme she has explored before, the relationship between artist and model, in which the former controls the latter and is the spectator, while the latter is powerless and is the spectacle. Here the statue/model turns the tables on the sculptor.

In the first part of the poem a series of images is presented in which Pygmalion is unable or unwilling to recognise that his demands on the statue are unwelcome: '*He will not touch me*, / but he did' (2–3), 'I lay still / as though I'd died. / He stayed' (5–7), 'He ran his clammy hands along my limbs. / I didn't shrink, / played statue, shtum' (23–5). The focus is not only on Pygmalion's inability to pick up significant clues, but also on the nature of his attraction to the statue. The suggestion is that while the statue remains unobtainable, she remains desirable. Pygmalion persists in his intentions, attempting to manipulate her; and the statue's lack of response, instead of dissuading him, has the opposite effect. He becomes more demanding, even cruel: 'He let his fingers sink into my flesh' (26), and 'His nails were claws' (32). The depiction of the relationship is uncomfortable. Her coldness, even lifelessness, seems to arouse the sculptor's interest. It is not a real flesh and blood woman that he wants, but some sexualised figure that he can control, like a rubber doll, a fetish: 'He propped me up on pillows' (34). This raises another issue about gender: the way in which, Duffy argues, women are **objectified** sexually.

The statue considers how else she might rid herself of Pygmalion's unwanted attentions. Being astute she chooses the opposite course of action to the one previously pursued and is thereby empowered. She becomes responsive, 'warm, like candle wax' (40), and builds to the point of orgasm: 'began to moan, / got hot, got wild, / arched, coiled, writhed' and then 'screamed my head off' (43–5, 48) in the full knowledge that her goal will be achieved. Once she expresses human emotions and feminine desires, wanting, for example, the sculptor to father a child – which we can also read as wanting commitment – she knows that he will lose interest. The poem ends with a rhyme and a **couplet**, signalling closure.

CHECK THE BOOK

Duffy's poem 'Standing Female Nude' in the volume of the same name (published in 1985) explores the relationship between the artist and the artist's model. Read it to compare its outcome with that of 'Pygmalion's Bride'.

CHECK THE BOOK

In Shakespeare's *The Winter's Tale* (*c.*1611), a statue reminiscent of Pygmalion's comes to life. The statue is of Hermione, who is thought to be dead.

CONTEXT

George Bernard Shaw (1856–1950) wrote the play *Pygmalion* (first performed in 1913). Set in Edwardian society a professor tries to transform a cockney flower seller into a lady. Shaw's version of the myth was adapted into the popular musical *My Fair Lady* (1956), which was made into a film in 1964.

CONTEXT

The term 'Rip Van Winkle' is used to refer to someone who is unaware of or out of touch with topical issues.

CONTEXT

Washington Irving (1783–1859) was an American writer of folk tales, biographies and essays. His most famous tales are 'Rip Van Winkle' and 'The Legend of Sleepy Hollow', from the collection *The Sketch Book*, written under the pseudonym Geoffrey Crayon (1819–20). It is worth reading 'Rip Van Winkle' to compare the characters with those in Duffy's poem.

MRS RIP VAN WINKLE

- Mrs Rip Van Winkle leads a new life while her husband is asleep.
- He has made sexual demands that she does not enjoy.
- Returning home one day, she discovers that he has woken up and wants to resume his sexual activities.

Mrs Rip Van Winkle has discovered a new life for herself, which includes painting and travel, while her husband is in a long deep sleep. She has reached late middle age and does not enjoy the sexual side of her relationship with him. But she returns home one day from her travels to find that he has woken. In his hand is a bottle of Viagra.

COMMENTARY

The tale 'Rip Van Winkle' is a good example of **intertextuality** and the adage that no story is a new one. The version that has entered popular American and European culture was written by the American writer Washington Irving in the early nineteenth century, though his story may have more than one source. Duffy has added another perspective to the tale with 'Mrs Rip Van Winkle'. In Irving's story a farmer escapes his shrewish wife to wander across the Catskill Mountains west of the Hudson River. After a series of adventures he falls asleep under a tree and sleeps for twenty years, waking up to a changed world. Duffy is no doubt familiar with this tale and is likely to have made a mental note of the nagging wife as a piece of **misogyny**. Irving's Rip Van Winkle is a dreamy character, unable to keep his own farm in shape. Much is made of his wife's accusations of idleness. He is, however, well liked by neighbours, particular female neighbours, again a point that Duffy may have noted, since in the poem she draws attention to Rip Van Winkle's sexual demands.

In Carol Ann Duffy's version, written in six **tercets**, Mrs Rip Van Winkle is cast as a middle-class housewife at odds with her husband and relieved to be rid of him. Although the poem is written in a comic style, it has an undercurrent of sadness, if not bleakness. After many years of what might be construed as sexual intimacy that she did not enjoy, she is left 'aching from head to foot' (3), though the image could also refer to a lifetime of drudgery, as she sinks 'into the still, deep waters of late middle age' (2).

There are various interpretations of sleep in fairy tales. In those rewritten as morality tales, sleep can represent indolence. But sometimes it can **symbolise** escape, and Duffy provides just this, not for a henpecked Rip Van Winkle but for the weary and put-upon wife. They are an ill-matched pair, and now that her husband is in semi-permanent slumber, her life takes on new meaning. Instead of 'exercise' (5), a reference to the sexual act, she prefers food, and indulges her love of painting and travel. Without him she blossoms. She visits the Leaning Tower of Pisa, the Pyramids, the Taj Mahal and the Niagara Falls. These are usually listed in one or other of the Seven Wonders of the World, ancient, medieval, modern or natural, and reveal not only how stultifying and limited Mrs Rip Van Winkle's life has been with her husband, but also what she regards as pleasure. Though the greatest pleasure of all, it seems, is 'saying a none-too-fond farewell to sex' (15).

With this thought, the reader is carried into the last verse, only to discover that unfortunately for Mrs Rip Van Winkle, Duffy chooses to follow the traditional tale. Her husband wakes up. After how long we do not know, but his sleep has refreshed him. This is not all. The poem ends with a **closed couplet** and **antithesis**. His wife returns one day with 'a pastel of Niagara' (17) to find him with an entirely different mindset: 'sitting up in bed rattling Viagra' (18).

GLOSSARY

10 **The Leaning Tower** (of Pisa) the circular bell tower of the cathedral in Pisa, Italy. It was built to be upright but began to lean during its construction from around 1173

11 **The Pyramids** ancient Egyptian tombs built for the pharaohs

continued

CONTEXT

In 'Rip Van Winkle', Irving refers to the old Dutch legends that were brought to America. Although the references are couched in fictional language, a link may exist between his tale and those from Dutch or German folklore.

CONTEXT

Another possible source for Irving's tale may be Diogenes Laertius' *Epimenides*, recorded around AD200. Epimenides is thought to be an ancient Greek philosopher and poet, around whom tales have been spun. Laertius records that he fell asleep for fifty-seven years in a sacred cave, and awoke with the gift of second sight or prophecy.

CONTEXT

Viagra is a drug used in the treatment of male impotency.

CONTEXT

Pieter Brueghel the Elder (*c.*1525–69) painted *Landscape with the Fall of Icarus* (1558) depicting Icarus disappearing into the sea. There is only a glimpse of him, however, as the main subjects of the painting, the ploughman and the shepherd, carry on with their work, unaware of the disaster.

CHECK THE BOOK

The modernist poet W. H. Auden (1907–73) took Brueghel the Elder's painting *Landscape with the Fall of Icarus* as stimulus for his poem 'Musée des Beaux Arts', noting: 'In Brueghel's *Icarus*, for instance: how everything turns away / Quite leisurely from the disaster'. This poem can be found in Auden's *Collected Shorter Poems 1927–1957* (1966).

GLOSSARY

11 **Taj Mahal** mausoleum built in Agra, India, between 1631 and 1653

17 **Niagara** (Falls) a series of gigantic waterfalls situated on the Niagara River between North America and Canada

MRS ICARUS

- Mrs Icarus recounts Icarus' attempts at flight.

Mrs Icarus describes watching her husband's attempts to fly – and is scathing about his failure.

COMMENTARY

Icarus is the son of Daedalus in Greek mythology. Both are imprisoned in Crete by King Minos, and Daedalus devises a means of escape by air, since there is no feasible escape by water. He fashions two sets of wings, one for himself and one for his son, with the command to Icarus that he should not fly too high. As father and son cross the Aegean, a ploughman and a shepherd look on, thinking that they must be seeing the gods. Icarus, emboldened by his success, flies too near the sun. His wings, which are held together by wax, melt, and he plunges into the Aegean.

The story has been handed down as a moral lesson about the dangers of pride or challenging the might of the gods. It is also echoed in the proverb 'Pride comes before a fall'. This is the central point of Duffy's poem, as told by Mrs Icarus. The image of Icarus taking to the air from a hill is reminiscent of the many eccentric attempts at human-powered flight, particularly in the nineteenth and early twentieth centuries. We suspect from the tone of the verse that Mrs Icarus has foreseen what will happen but is ignored by her husband anyway. It also conjures up pictures of wives in general having to endure their husbands' hobbies and obsessions such as football, fishing, trainspotting, and so forth.

The five-line verse is written as a joke and comes alive when heard as a **performance poem**. English is a heavily accented language, and the solid English thump in 'hillock' and 'pillock' reminds us of comic verse or a nursery rhyme. The poem could also be described as an **insult poem** (see the commentary on 'Mrs Darwin' in **Detailed summaries** for further discussion on the insult poem).

CHECK THE BOOK

The American poet William Carlos Williams (1883–1963) also takes Brueghel the Elder's painting as stimulus for his poem 'Landscape With the Fall of Icarus', making a similar observation to Auden: 'there was / a splash quite unnoticed'. This poem can be found in his *Collected Poems II: 1939–1962.*

FRAU FREUD

- Freud's wife is presented as a public speaker addressing a female audience.
- She describes her husband's penis in unflattering slang, undermining his manhood and his theories.

Frau Freud is the long-suffering wife of the famous psychoanalyst Sigmund Freud, and here she is cast as a commanding public speaker addressing a female audience. She simultaneously **satirises** her husband's penis – the essence of his manhood – and his theories in slang, as a series of unflattering **synonyms**.

COMMENTARY

Duffy has a great deal of fun at Freud's expense here, giving Frau Freud the opportunity to say exactly how she feels about a principal subject of the great man's theories: the penis. For Freud the sexual drive – libido – is central to human existence as a means of bodily pleasure. We suppress many of our urges in our unconscious minds, which are expressed in dreams or slips of the tongue, sometimes called Freudian slips.

Just as Freud possesses authority, so does Frau Freud. 'Ladies,' she begins, followed by a pause. A clear image of a mature, robust and experienced wife springs into view as she addresses an audience of women only, perhaps from a podium, or even at a Women's Institute meeting. The address is polite and formal and the pause used for effect. She continues: 'for argument's sake, let us say' – much as a speaker might do at a symposium of Freudian psychoanalysts. What follows, by contrast, is a list of slang words

CONTEXT

Freud (1856–1939) is considered to be one of the most influential thinkers of the modern era. He is best known for his investigations into the workings of the unconscious mind, and particularly for his work on repression and sexual drives. Freudian expressions such as 'ego' have entered mainstream **discourse**.

CHECK THE BOOK

Read Avril Horner's comment on 'Frau Freud', in which she refers to 'vaginal envy' and the way in which the poem 'undermines the supposed objectivity of psychoanalytic discourse', in '"Small Female Skull": patriarchy and philosophy in the poetry of Carol Ann Duffy' in *The Poetry of Carol Ann Duffy: 'Choosing Tough Words'*, edited by Angelica Michelis and Antony Rowland (2003), p. 113.

for the penis, sometimes told in a surfeit of rhyme and lumpy **dipodic metre** similar to a comic song or nursery rhyme. The third and fourth lines in particular are reminiscent of such nursery rhymes as 'A dillar, a dollar, a ten o'clock scholar'. The poem is also written in fourteen lines as a **sonnet**, or rather a mockery of one. This irreverence works to cut both Freud's theories down to size, so to speak, and his own penis, as we shall see by the end of the poem. Indeed, this endless repetition of slang for the penis suggests that her husband, to use his own **psychoanalytical** term, is fixated with it. She, on the other hand, is well balanced, if long-suffering: 'Don't get me wrong, I've no axe to grind / with the snake in the trousers' (10–11). She simply wants to point out that Freud has misinterpreted female sexuality.

Freud's theory of penis envy, in which the adolescent girl subconsciously realises that she lacks a penis and is thus envious, and which he sees as a critical point in female sexual identity, has caused great contention and annoyance among many **feminists**. There is a view that his theories, when applied to women, cannot be trusted because he was a Victorian patriarch and paterfamilias – head of the family – and unable to see things from a woman's perspective. Not only this, but his theories give credibility to an already **patriarchal** society. In her summing up Frau Freud declares that 'the average penis [is] not pretty' (13), and notes 'the squint of its envious solitary eye' (14). A feminist might argue that Duffy in this poem cleverly subverts Freud's notion of penis envy, so that it is the penis which becomes envious of the clitoris. In this reading, to regard one's penis as so inadequate can only evoke 'pity' (14), claims Frau Freud, thereby attacking both her husband's theory and his own penis in one.

GLOSSARY

6 **Ms M. Lewinsky** Monica Lewinsky was the young White House intern and lover of Bill Clinton (b.1946), American president between 1993 and 2001

SALOME

- Salome wakes to find yet again a strange man next to her in bed.
- She comments on his manly appearance, kisses him, then calls for her maid to bring breakfast and vows to give up her vices.
- When she pulls back the sheets she reveals the stranger's head on a platter.

Salome wakes with a hangover. Next to her in bed is a strange man, not an unusual occurrence. She studies him, notes his manly beauty and kisses him, though he does not respond. Unable to remember his name she calls her maid for tea and toast, vows to give up her hedonistic life, and decides to send the stranger on his way. When she pulls back the sheets she reveals his severed head on a platter.

COMMENTARY

A first reading of this free verse poem presents us with a young woman whose taste for the common vices of drinking, smoking and sex mirrors that of contemporary young women as depicted in the media or in popular fiction. Once alerted to the twist at the end, a second reading reveals much earlier that Salome is no Bridget Jones. In the first verse, when she studies the man lying next to her in bed, the images resonate with meaning. The 'dark hair, rather matted', the 'reddish beard', the 'very deep lines round the eyes, / from pain, I'd guess' and 'a beautiful crimson mouth' all imply blood and suffering (6–10). When she kisses him at the end of the first verse and he is 'Colder than pewter' (13), we know it is a corpse – or to be gruesomely precise, less than one – lying next to Salome. She cannot remember this stranger's name; her unnerving detachment shows no emotional connection. She does not seek comfort from casual sex. For Salome it is only a brief contract with a stranger, for her own purposes. She runs through a list of names in her mind to recall who this stranger might be. They are all Apostles of Jesus.

In the Bible Salome requests the head of the imprisoned John the Baptist after performing a dance for Herod Antipas, her stepfather. John, the prophet who foretold the coming of Christ, is brought to

CONTEXT

In the biblical story Herodias incites her daughter, Salome, to request the head of John the Baptist when offered a choice of reward for her dancing (see Mark 6:17–28 and Matthew 14:1–12). Salome was an actual historical figure, the granddaughter of Herod the Great, who was responsible for the Massacre of the Innocents.

CONTEXT

Bridget Jones is a fictional character created by Helen Fielding. Stories written in the form of a diary and published in the *Independent* and *Daily Telegraph* recounted the life and relationship traumas of Bridget Jones, a single woman in her thirties living in London who was desperate to find true love. In 1996 the full-length novel *Bridget Jones's Diary* was published.

CONTEXT

Wilde's *Salomé* was published in 1894 in England, though first published in France a year earlier. Aubrey Beardsley, well known for his erotic drawings, drew the illustrations.

CHECK THE BOOK

For a very useful discussion of gender, sexuality and death and the figure of Salome see pp. 49–50 and pp. 159–60 of *Consorting with Angels: Essays on Modern Women Poets* by Deryn Rees-Jones (2005).

CONTEXT

The seductive dance of the seven veils has long been connected to Salome and illustrates her erotic allure. It occurs in Richard Strauss' *Salomé* (1905), an opera based on a German translation of Wilde's play, although the dance remains unnamed in the latter.

Salome as a head on a platter. However, the poem in its depiction of Salome's character and the kiss in line 12 owes more to Oscar Wilde's play *Salomé*. In Wilde's play, when John the Baptist spurns her advances she demands his head. This is the vengeful Salome of the poem. Instead of the knowing young girl depicted in the first reading of the poem we have a serial killer, a figure generally associated with men, not women: 'I'd done it before / (and doubtless I'll do it again, / sooner or later)' (1–3). The innocent clatter of the maid contrasts with Salome's guilt. Her casual turning away from the scene of the crime to order breakfast suggests alienation, just as the head separated from its body does. Salome's 'night on the batter' (23) refers to assault as well as sex, while the **colloquialism** 'I needed to clean up my act' (25) has an **ironic** twist. She must clean away the blood after the act of violence, as well as 'clean up' her life.

Salome's motives for killing are not explicit. We might see her as a **symbolic** avenging angel, fighting the forces of **patriarchy**, much like Duffy's Queen Herod, but it is less clear-cut in this poem. There is no female collective agenda as there is with Queen Herod and the three wise Queens. There are some small clues that might imply a similar but more personal motive. The man is referred to as a 'beater or biter' (30). Does this suggests Salome experiences physical violence and perversion at the hands of men when they 'come' (31) – that is, at the point of orgasm? This is also the point when she indulges in her 'slaughter' (31). But there are no other images that suggest she is abused. At the end of the poem she displays her enjoyment of murder and transgression and her lack of remorse: 'lamb to the slaughter' (31) has biblical **connotations**. Christ was the Lamb of God, atoning for the sins of humanity. Is the dead stranger being made to atone for his sins against her and of men against women? We can speculate what her motives might be, while remembering that there may be none. Certainly there is no apology for her behaviour as she uses sex to dupe men. Sex, death and pleasure are bound together. In the very last lines she displays her gruesome anticipation at seeing the dismembered head:

> I saw my eyes glitter.
> I flung back the sticky red sheets,
> and there, like I said – and ain't life a bitch –
> was his head on a platter. (33–6)

There is irony in the use of the word 'bitch'. It can be an especially abusive sexual term for a woman. Here it is said with conviction and hatred as Salome triumphantly throws it back at the male as a demonstration of her power.

THE KRAY SISTERS

- The infamous underworld criminals the Kray twins are depicted as the Kray sisters.
- It is clear that the sisters are female supporters of the women's movement.

The Kray twins, Ronnie and Reggie, were at the head of the criminal underworld in the 1960s. In the poem they have been transformed into the Kray sisters. While the twins' notoriety has been maintained, and their brutal activities are similar, the sisters are fighting in the cause of **feminism** and the poem is a reminiscence of the sisters' past lives.

COMMENTARY

The poem opens with the sisters recalling the early days of their gangland life and the impression they made on the locality. This image immediately strikes a tension between the masculine and the feminine. The sisters have all the thrusting ambition of the gangster, in their expensive Savile Row suits – 'whistles and flutes' (3) – translated into a bold **feminine** stance to 'flatter' their 'thr'penny bits' (4). They conjure up in the reader's mind the image of cross-dressing, either as women dressed as men or vice versa. Appropriately, their reminiscences are sentimental in tone: 'Oh, London, London, / London Town' (7–8), since sentimentality often goes hand in hand with brutality in the gangster's world.

Throughout the poem, the sisters have one voice, united against the forces of patriarchy, and are indistinguishable, one from the other, which serves to present a single voice for the **dramatic monologue**. This avoids the use of dialogue and accentuates their sisterhood and commitment to feminism. It also blurs the distinction between the sisters – 'No one could tell us apart' (5) – as it did the Krays, who were identical twins, and who used this to avoid detection and prosecution.

CONTEXT

Ronnie (1933–95) and Reggie Kray (1933–2000) were notorious gangsters in the East End of London, whose methods of intimidation and violence placed them at the head of organised crime in 1960s Britain. They opened clubs and casinos and also had links with the Mafia. They were convicted of murder in 1969 and sentenced to life imprisonment.

QUESTION

What might the Kray sisters be saying about the state of feminism in the late twentieth century in this poem?

CHECK THE BOOK

The Profession of Violence: The Rise and Fall of the Kray Twins by John Pearson (1972, revised edition 1995) gives a detailed and chilling account of the criminals' lives.

CONTEXT

Emmeline Pankhurst (1858–1928) was a leading suffragette who set up the Women's Social and Political Union (WSPU) in 1903. With her daughter Christabel, she campaigned for the vote for women, which was initially granted in 1918 to women of thirty and over, and in 1928 to women of twenty-one and over.

CONTEXT

Gay icons are usually entertainers or celebrities who have known tragedy or survived personal difficulties, or whose emotional impact strikes a chord with the gay and lesbian community.

CONTEXT

Vita Sackville West (1892–1962) was a poet and novelist; Violet Trefusis (1894–1972), a writer and socialite, was her one-time lover.

In the second verse they recollect their childhood and their initiation into feminism while sitting at their grandmother's skirts (19–20), and learning the story of 'Emmeline's Army' and other heroines of the movement. In reality the Kray twins were very close to their mother, Violet, who heavily influenced them. Here she is depicted as the sisters' grandmother, 'Cannonball Vi' (the Kray twins' grandfather was Jimmy 'Cannonball' Lee). In the poem Vi is a suffragette, and is compared to Emily Davison (1872–1913), who was killed when she threw herself in front of King George V's horse at the 1913 Derby. 'Cannonball Vi' (18), however, tough and ruthless, manages to knock out the horse with a well-judged punch 'for the cause' (a further reference to the Kray twins' grandfather, who was a boxer). Throughout the poem Duffy is playing with the boundaries of gender and sexual identity. There are constant parallels between the male Kray twins and the female sisters, who, as we have seen, have masculine tendencies. In life Ronnie Kray was openly homosexual while his brother is reputed to have been bisexual, and most of the celebrities listed in the poem are gay and lesbian icons.

The sisters' education turns into 'a vocation' (27) in the third verse. They pursue 'respect' (27) for their gender and, as the Kray twins tortured and humiliated their victims, so the sisters set about emasculating men in support of the feminist cause, 'with simply a menacing look, a threatening word' (29). They turn to past figures such as the lesbians 'Vita and Violet' (35) for their inspiration and to consolidate the movement, much as all groups do who are fighting a cause.

In the fourth verse they remember the mistakes they made, and recall allowing into their movement women who became embroiled with men. This apparent act of betrayal also highlights how they believe men should be treated: as sexual objects, as women can be in the real world, particularly the underworld. Serious relationships with men are regarded as consorting with the enemy, because men are dispensable: 'Rule Number One – / A boyfriend's for Christmas, not just for life' (42–3). At their first club – aptly named 'Ballbreakers' (45) – they provide 'Protection' (48) for women. This means the literal protection of vulnerable women, and possibly protection against pregnancy (contraception), and also refers

euphemistically to protection provided by gangsters, which in reality is extortion. By the fifth verse they have consolidated their empire, moving to a more elegant, upmarket club where they consort with the stars. They reminisce about '*the Good Old Days*' (59), a reference to a popular programme which ran from the 1950s to the 1980s, and the letters they receive from their grateful female supporters.

In the final verse the sisters recall themselves at the peak of their power, idolised at their club where they are sufficiently powerful to lean on 'Sinatra to sing for free' (64). Again the poet is playing with gender, since this refers to both Frank Sinatra (1915–98), who was rumoured to have had links to the Mafia, and his daughter Nancy (b.1940), who made famous the song sung at the club: 'These Boots Are Made for Walkin''. The image of 'her beautiful throat' (70) can also refer to either celebrity; the use of the female pronoun 'her' is commonly used to refer to men in the gay world. The poem ends with lines from the song, re-emphasising the sisters' sentimental and brutal commitment to the cause as the boots trample over some fictitious male. This is the way in which the sisters would wish to be remembered.

The poem is littered with phrases from cockney rhyming slang, the meanings of which are themselves sometimes slang in mainstream culture, for example 'orchestra stalls' (30) to mean balls (testes). Although used to comic effect in the poem, there is also a serious point being made. Subcultures usually maintain a **vernacular** as a code of secrecy, which separates them from the mainstream. Here this has the effect of accentuating the subversive nature of the Kray sisters' activities in their support of the feminist cause. There are other techniques used to create comic effects in the poem. **Alliteration** is one. Duffy also captures the **timbre** of the Krays' speech, partly by using pause, **caesura** and sometimes rhyme. This has the triple effect of controlling the pace of the poem, affirming the credibility of the speech as well as presenting a comic depiction. The following example illustrates these four techniques and gives another vivid picture of the Kray sisters as they would wish to be remembered: 'up West to a club; to order up bubbly, the best, / in a bucket of ice. Garland singing that night. Nice' (11–12).

CONTEXT

All the women mentioned in lines 55–7 came to fame in the 1960s and are all gay icons or sympathetic to the gay community (see the glossary for further information).

CHECK THE FILM

In 1990 the film *The Krays*, written by Philip Ridley, was made starring the brothers Gary and Martin Kemp of the band Spandau Ballet and directed by Peter Medak.

CONTEXT

Judy Garland (1922–69) was an American singer and actress. She was able to convey great emotion, partly because of the nature of her voice. Her private life was largely tragic, and she is probably the principal gay icon in the poem. She knew the Kray twins, as did the British actresses Barbara Windsor (b.1937) – **'Babs'** (56) – and Diana Dors (1931–84).

CHECK THE BOOK

Wise Children (1991) by Angela Carter is similar in tone to the 'The Kray Sisters' in its use of **colloquialism**. The characters and content also share similarities; *Wise Children* tells the history of identical twins Dora and Nora, and is told from the perspective of old age. It includes elements of both comedy and **tragedy**.

CONTEXT

During his career, Elvis Presley (1935–77) recorded over four hundred and fifty original songs. In his later years Elvis became isolated and depressed, had a poor diet and became heavily dependent on prescription drugs. There is a generally held view that he regretted the course of his career, which, though successful, shifted from rhythm and blues in his early years to sentimental films and ballads.

GLOSSARY

20 **Vera Lynn** singer famous during the Second World War

55 **Germaine** Germaine Greer (b.1939) leading feminist and academic

Bardot Brigitte Bardot (b.1934), French film actress

56 **Twiggy** (b.1949) British model

Lulu (b.1948) British pop singer

Dusty Dusty Springfield (1939–99), British pop singer

Yoko Yoko Ono (b.1933), Japanese singer, wife of John Lennon

Bassey Shirley Bassey (b.1937), British singer

57 **Sandy** Sandie Shaw (b.1947), British pop singer

ELVIS'S TWIN SISTER

- Elvis Presley's twin sister describes her life as a nun.
- She works in the nunnery garden as Sister Presley.
- She describes the unassuming clothes she wears and how her adoption of a simple life has led to happiness.

Elvis' fictional twin sister describes her life, tending the plants in the nunnery garden. She is Sister Presley, admired by the Reverend Mother for the way she wiggles her hips like her famous brother. In her life of worship and simple attire she has achieved a state of grace, and her previous life of loneliness and heartbreak are long gone.

COMMENTARY

Carol Ann Duffy takes the **iconic** figure of Elvis Presley and creates a playfully **satirical** poem. Instead of creating a speaker that is a wife or lover, as she does in most of the poems, here the speaker is Elvis' fictional female twin. And she is not only a woman, but she leads a simple happy existence, in direct opposition to that of her brother's. There are many comparisons in the poem. Where her life is frugal, his was indulgent. Where she nurtures, he was self-destructive. Where she has companionship, he was lonely. There are many precise references to Elvis Presley in the poem. The **epigraph** is the first. 'Are You Lonesome Tonight?' is one of his most famous songs, and the quip from Madonna in which she audaciously compares herself to Elvis helped to promote her career.

The American accent of the southern states in the first line of the poem – 'y'all' – is Elvis' voice and dialect. He often used the expression when speaking to an audience, and the line 'the way I move my hips' (9) is a reference to Elvis' gyrations on stage. In response to this, the phrase 'Elvis the Pelvis' emerged in the British popular press of the 1950s. Against these references run the Catholic ones. Sister Presley prays 'for the immortal soul / of rock 'n' roll' (4–5), calling attention to the near religious fervour of Elvis' more adoring fans. It is also an **irony** in view of the condemnation heaped on Elvis when he first started his career. In America his music and performance were considered by the establishment, in particular the religious establishment, to be a corrupting influence on the young. The Gregorian chant '*Pascha nostrum immolatus est …*' (13), which refers to Christ as the sacrificial lamb, is here used as a **metaphor** for the way in which Elvis and his talent were squandered by some close to him, largely for commercial gain. While Sister Presley lives in 'a land of grace' (23), is blessed and at peace through her religion, Elvis achieved no such state in his lifetime and died young. Ironically, however, his mansion was called Graceland. Sister Presley has left behind loneliness and sorrow – 'Lonely Street' and 'Heartbreak Hotel' (29–30), two references to the Elvis song 'Heartbreak Hotel' – and by recovering his 'trademark', his 'slow lopsided smile' (24), she restores the image of the youthful Elvis, whose extraordinary potential once seemed assured.

The structure of the poem, six **quintains**, has an ordered pattern that suits the life of Sister Presley. In contrast, the **full rhyme**, for example 'hues' and 'shoes' (15 and 20); **double rhyme**, 'mother' and 'brother' (8 and 10); **slant rhyme**, 'keys' and 'shoes' (18 and 20); and other variations suit the music of rock 'n' roll. And the irregularity of the rhyme throughout the verses suits the way rock 'n' roll challenged the existing norms in 1950s society.

CONTEXT

Elvis had a twin brother, Jessie Garon, who was stillborn.

CHECK THE NET

Conspiracy theories surrounding the deaths of famous people are common in contemporary society. The theory that Elvis Presley is still alive was promulgated soon after his death. With the development of the Internet such theories can now be circulated very rapidly. For more information about 'sightings' of Elvis since his death, together with details about his life and recordings, go to **www.wikipedia.org** and search for Elvis Presley.

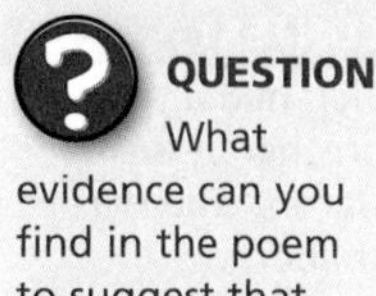

QUESTION What evidence can you find in the poem to suggest that Elvis and Sister Presley are different sides of the same person?

CONTEXT

Elvis started singing in his church choir, and during the course of his career he released a number of gospel albums, including *His Hand in Mine* and *Peace in the Valley*.

CONTEXT

The legend of Pope Joan was widely believed during the Middle Ages and was recorded by the Polish chronicler Martin of Opava in the thirteenth century. He notes that Pope Joan was known as John Anglicus, who rose through the ranks to become Pope. Some historians believe the tale was devised as a **satire**.

In the last verse Duffy focuses on the bizarre theory, popular among some of Elvis' diehard fans, that their **icon** is still alive. So who is Sister Presley? The clue comes in the last verse of the poem when she says: 'I'm alive and well' (27). For 'twin sister' we can read 'Elvis reborn'. Elvis was not only a sex symbol, but was reputed to be something of a womaniser. In the poem Duffy is inviting us to have fun with the **feminist** idea that his **alter ego** is a contented female, living in a community of women.

GLOSSARY

11	**Gregorian chant** chant sung in the Catholic Church by monks and nuns
13	***Pascha nostrum immolatus est …*** Christ at Easter has been sacrificed for us
16	**wimple** a piece of cloth draped around the head, framing the face, as worn by nuns
17	**rosary** a string of beads used to count prayers as they are said in Catholicism
20	**blue suede shoes** a song sung by Elvis (recorded in 1956)
22	**Graceland** Elvis' estate in Memphis, Tennessee, now a museum

POPE JOAN

- Joan has become Pope, the head of the Catholic Church.
- She describes the religious rituals that confirm her position.
- She also says that she no longer believes.
- The only thing that is miraculous is the birth of her child.

Carol Ann Duffy rewrites the legend of Pope Joan, a popular tale from the Middle Ages in which a woman disguised as a man holds the papal office for over two years. Joan describes her venerable position and the religious rituals that confirm her status, comparing herself to men. But she no longer believes in the Church's teachings. For Joan the birth of her child is the nearest she has come to the miraculous.

COMMENTARY

Duffy's depictions of Pope Joan in St Peter's Square ministering to her followers in the first verses are graphic. They not only conjure up the mystical experience felt by the faithful, the 'fervent crowds' (7), but also indicate the hierarchical nature of the Church, with its 'Vicar of Rome' (12), the Pope being 'nearer to heaven' (10) than anyone else, followed by cardinals and other officers of the Church. In reality a female Pope would be highly unlikely. Apart from Reverend Mothers, who are the heads of convents, women are not permitted to hold office in the Catholic faith. Duffy, herself brought up a Catholic, though no longer practising, would be well aware of both the rituals and the position of women in the Church.

CONTEXT

In 1601 the legend of Pope Joan was declared untrue by Pope Clement VIII and the bust of her either destroyed or re-carved to depict a male figure (for more information see *The Oxford Dictionary of Popes* by J. N. D. Kelly, 1986).

Duffy's rewriting of the legend of Pope Joan is very close to the original storyline. In the legend Pope Joan gives birth in a narrow lane during a religious procession and inevitably is disgraced. In the poem it is this lowly road in which the religious experience, the 'miracle', takes place. When Joan addresses the women of the poem, the 'daughters or brides of the Lord' (20), she makes clear that miraculous power resides not in the Church but in the creation of a child.

The images are also religious or biblical. The lowly position of the 'blue-green snakes of smoke' (5) is reminiscent of the serpent in the Garden of Eden in Genesis who tempted Eve and became the lowliest of creatures. Similarly, the image of God's hand 'lifting me, flinging me down' (24), while an image of the act of giving birth, is as much like God casting out Lucifer, the fallen angel from heaven and sometimes depicted as the serpent. It is also a **metaphor** for Joan being cast out of the Church.

CONTEXT

Images of Lucifer or Satan are not always entirely religious, but are mixed with medieval myth.

So the 'miracle' (29) Joan speaks of is not a religious birth, and she leaves pomp and circumstance behind to embrace the ordinary road. To give birth is a natural experience equally available to all women, be they Pope or not, and one that a man cannot share. Pope Joan's loss of faith in the mystical has been replaced by the affirmation of women's physical experience.

CONTEXT

The poem is also reminiscent of Joan of Arc or Jeanne d'Arc (c.1412–31) in its depiction of a powerful woman. Joan of Arc claimed to have seen religious visions in which she was told to rid France of English interference. The uncrowned French king sent her to Orleans, where she lifted a siege. She was convicted of heresy and burned at the stake by the English. She was canonised in 1920.

GLOSSARY

1	**transubstantiate** convert bread and wine into the body and blood of Christ at consecration (in Christianity)
2	**unleavened bread** bread made without yeast
4	**frankincense** a resin burnt as incense; used in the Catholic Church
15	**in nomine patris et filii et spiritus sancti** in the name of the father (God), son (Jesus Christ), and the Holy Spirit

PENELOPE

- Penelope waits for her husband, Odysseus, to return from his travels.
- She takes up the art of embroidery.
- Finally Odysseus returns, but he is too late. Penelope has changed.

Penelope begins her long wait looking 'along the road' (1), watching for some signs of her husband's return. Six months pass and she takes up embroidery as a diversion. This becomes her main preoccupation and she weaves beautiful pictures. When her husband finally returns, he is no longer welcome. Penelope has developed a new perspective on the world.

CONTEXT

Odysseus is the hero of Homer's *Odyssey*, one of the great epic poems of ancient Greece, probably written between 800 and 200BC. It is mainly concerned with the events of Odysseus' ten-year journey after the ten-year Trojan War.

COMMENTARY

In Homer's *Odyssey*, Penelope waits twenty years for her husband, Odysseus, to return from a lifetime of voyaging. She successfully fends off several suitors and avoids remarriage, although she does become discontent with her lot towards the end of her wait. She is, however, the **symbol** of faithfulness, and a traditional rendering of the myth would have focused on this symbol. Duffy's poem, written in five verses each of nine lines, presents Penelope as a rather different kind of sailor's wife. She ruminates on the past, weaving her own history into her embroidery, which becomes the principal **metaphor** for her life. It is her main preoccupation, and from it she learns not only wisdom but discovers her own creative power. At first she recalls her childhood, 'I sewed a girl'

(12), and tries to capture its ephemeral quality, as suggested in the image 'running after childhood's bouncing ball' (14). The colours she chooses possess the hopefulness of youth – greens and pink – but already there is the image of disappointment in the grey she also picks.

As her creativity grows, so does her awareness of her state. Both are captured in the **simile** of her thimble 'like an acorn' (19), growing. Using her skill with the needle, she depicts herself as a young woman in love with Odysseus, 'heroism's boy' (23). She loses herself in her creation and also in the memory of her love. The **alliteration** in line 25 is cleverly chosen so that the 'love' and 'lust' of youthful passion slips into 'loss' and 'lessons learnt' – into wisdom.

In verse four, by which time Odysseus has been absent for many years, Penelope has no desire to replace him with other men. She has learned independence and how to cherish it. In the myth the suitors must string an especially difficult bow accurately to win her hand in marriage. The task allows Penelope to gain time, in the hope that Odyssesus will return. In the poem her task of embroidery acts in a similar way, but to preserve her independence. She wears widow's weeds as a disguise for her lack of interest in her suitors, and at night she unpicks her work. The image that follows, of the moon fraying, is telling. It is a metaphor for disenchantment. Penelope has become not cynical but knowing about love.

As we move into the final verse, there is perhaps a touch of poignancy in her acknowledgement that the river she creates in her embroidery will 'never reach the sea' (38) – never reach Odysseus in a fulfilling relationship. Nonetheless, she does not wish to change her life. She has reached, after twenty years, an equilibrium, 'self-contained, absorbed, content' (41), and is no longer the wife who waits. So much so, that when her husband returns, 'his far-too-late familiar tread' becomes a threat (43). In the last line of the poem the powerful image is both a creative and a destructive act: 'I licked my scarlet thread / and aimed it surely at the middle of the needle's eye once more' (44–5). The scarlet thread can be seen as a metaphor for a weapon: 'scarlet' signals blood, the 'thread' a spear or arrow which, with her skill perfected, is aimed at the

CONTEXT

Embroidery is often a feature of women's art. It is included in Judy Chicago's famous work *The Dinner Party* (1974–79), an installation that depicts place settings on a triangular table for thirty-nine women from history and mythology. Hundreds of other women's names are written across the floor.

CHECK THE NET

'Waiting and hoping: the experience of women whose loved ones went to sea' is an informative article by Margarette Lincoln on sailors' wives and how they adapt to their circumstances. Use an Internet search engine and search for the author's name and the article's title.

'middle', the heart. More broadly, we can say that Penelope dispenses with Odysseus through finding her own creative power.

MRS BEAST

- Mrs Beast says that a woman would be better off with a beast as a lover.
- The Beast does as she says.
- She plays poker with other powerful women, and recalls women who have suffered.
- She reveals that she is the less committed in her relationship with the Beast.

CONTEXT

All the women mentioned in the first verse are renowned for their beauty. The Queen of Sheba was the ruler of the Sabeans, who occupied a kingdom in North Africa; in the Bible she visits Solomon, hearing of his wisdom. According to Ethiopian tradition, the couple married and their son founded the Ethiopian royal dynasty. Juliet is the heroine of Shakespeare's *Romeo and Juliet*, a tale of two 'star-crossed' lovers. Nefertiti was the wife of the Egyptian pharaoh Amenhotep IV; her name means 'the beautiful one is come'. *Mona Lisa* is Leonardo da Vinci's famous portrait of an enigmatic, smiling lady. Greta Garbo (1905–90) was a reclusive Hollywood actress.

Mrs Beast addresses the reader, saying that rather than take a man as a lover, a woman would be better off with a beast. As an experienced woman, she arrives at the house of the Beast, and there she finds that he will meet her needs and remain servile. A number of powerful women are introduced, as the speaker describes the poker games they play. Together they recall those women less fortunate than themselves who have suffered in a male world. The speaker finally notes that she, not the male Beast, will be the one to give less emotional commitment in the relationship.

COMMENTARY

Duffy immediately refers to legends and fairy tales at the beginning of this poem, and in doing so draws attention to the **intertextuality** of the volume as a whole. 'I'll put them straight' (2), claims Mrs Beast, meaning that she will expose the stereotypical figures of these stories. She points to examples of famous female **icons** – for example Helen of Troy, the most beautiful of women in Greek mythology; Egypt's Queen Cleopatra; the Queen of Sheba; Greta Garbo – who a **feminist** would claim are objects of male desire, and as such are **patriarchal constructs**. Women, we can assume, are also susceptible to these constructs, in so far as women strive to be beautiful in the hope that their prince will come – the message of many fairy tales. But, says Mrs Beast in her knowing tone, 'when you stare / into my face' (2–3), 'think again' (6). She has another version of events, and takes 'The Little Mermaid' (6) as an example to illustrate her point. In Hans Christian Andersen's tale the Little Mermaid is steadfast and true, willing to endure everything – pain, loss of home and identity – for the love of her prince. In the poem she is depicted as a self-abusive victim, transforming her body for her 'pretty boy' (10) who, like all men of his type, will ultimately leave her. Mrs Beast's profound cynicism leads her to dispense advice as a mature woman: 'find yourself a Beast' rather than a man, she says (14).

As an independent woman of means, she is not prepared to accommodate patriarchy. The Beast is only too aware of his bestiality and undesirability and fawns on her. In this respect his depiction follows that of the fairy tale 'Beauty and the Beast', in which the Beast is humiliated by his appearance, only wanting a beautiful princess to come along and transform him into a man. Here, however, there is no attempt at **transformation**. The Beast remains bestial: 'he steamed in his pelt, / ugly as sin' (31–2). But, like Delilah's Samson, he is nonetheless intensely masculine in his physicality, if not in his role. So too is Mrs Beast intensely male, and this is where Duffy plays with gender roles. Mrs Beast has the controlling hand. She plays poker, typically a male game, and turns the Beast into a subservient domestic, typically a female role, making him wash the sheets 'Twice' (38). The Beast is required to meet her every need, and she treats him without compassion.

The green baize poker table is depicted in the fourth verse. Around it sit Mrs Beast and her companions. They are a strange mix, at once powerful, beautiful women from 'a hard school' (48), reminding us of a scene from a gangster movie, or Duffy's poem 'The Kray Sisters', and also grotesque comic characters. There are **allusions** to mythology, fairy tales and freak shows. The **imagery** is rich and irreverent, and the 'wonderful women' (52) have all chosen outsiders as husbands: 'the Woman / who Married a Minotaur, Goldilocks, the Bride / of the Bearded Lesbian, Frau Yellow Dwarf' and, as Mrs Beast archly declares, 'Moi' (49–51). Duffy depicts the smoky room, the growing tension, the bluff, slang and other colourful **clichés** from a typical poker game. Significantly the Bride of the Bearded Lesbian wins, underscoring the rejection of the traditional heterosexual relationship in the poem.

CHECK THE BOOK

With 'The Courtship of Mr Lyon' and 'The Tiger's Bride' in *The Bloody Chamber and Other Stories* (1979), Angela Carter offers two different takes on the story of 'Beauty and the Beast'.

CONTEXT

Duffy and Adrian Henri collaborated to produce a poetry pamphlet entitled *Beauty and the Beast* in 1977.

CONTEXT

Ashputtel and Rapunzel are both characters in fairy tales by the Brothers Grimm – 'Ashputtel' is a variation on 'Cinderella'.
In a story by Charles Perrault, Bluebeard is a violent nobleman who murders his wives.

CHECK THE BOOK

Auden writes: 'If equal affection cannot be, / Let the more loving one be me' ('The More Loving One' can be found in his *Collected Shorter Poems 1927–1957*).

CONTEXT

Demeter is depicted as the giver of seasons in the 'Homeric Hymns' (so called because they were once attributed to Homer), in which individual gods are celebrated, including Persephone. Demeter and Persephone are also figures in the Eleusinian mysteries.

Behind these poker players, however, appear the 'ghosts' of past women, all tragic, all 'unable to win', whom Mrs Beast and her companions respectfully acknowledge (70–6). Moved by the moment, Mrs Beast retires – after tyrannically sending away the Beast – and muses on 'the captive beautiful, / the wives, those less fortunate than we' (87–8), a clear reference to the long-suffering women and wives in *The World's Wife*. In a final defiant gesture Mrs Beast identifies the critical nub of the poem: her need for revenge against the heterosexual male who brings less emotional commitment to a relationship: 'Bring me the Beast for the night. / Bring me the wine-cellar key. Let the less-loving one be me' (91–2). The last few words are also an **ironic** reference to a line in the W. H. Auden poem 'The More Loving One'. Duffy reverses the sentiment, replacing 'more' with 'less', so emphasising Mrs Beast's female dominance.

GLOSSARY

28 **Châteaux Margaux '54** wine from the Médoc in France

50 **Minotaur** a beast – part man, part bull – in Greek mythology

Goldilocks main character in the fairy tale 'Goldilocks and the Three Bears'

53 **Five and Seven Card Stud … Draw** poker games

73 **Bessie Smith** (1894–1937) black American blues singer

78 ***Fay Wray*** (1907–2004) actress who played Ann Darrow in the 1933 film *King Kong*

87 **rosary** prayer beads in Catholicism

DEMETER

- It is winter. Demeter awaits the return of her daughter, Persephone.
- As Persephone returns, she brings the spring, and with it hope.

In this short poem, the last in the collection, Demeter is in the grip of winter, awaiting the return of Persephone. Demeter contrasts the barren winter months with the healing power of spring and the fertility and hope that Persephone represents.

COMMENTARY

In Greek mythology Demeter is the mother goddess of corn, the fertilising principle of nature. When Hades abducts Persephone and takes her to the underworld to be his wife, Demeter plunges the earth into endless winter. Persephone is finally returned to Demeter and the earth, but she can only stay for eight months of the year. While in the underworld Persephone had eaten four (sometimes the number is given as six) seeds from the fruit of the pomegranate – in some accounts the **symbol** of marriage – so she is obliged to spend the remaining four months with Hades. Hence the Greek myth of Demeter and Persephone depicts three fruitful seasons – spring, summer and autumn – when Persephone is on earth, and one barren season, winter, when she must return to the underworld.

The opening images of the poem see Demeter joyless in her 'cold stone room' (2). She chooses 'tough words, granite, flint, / to break the ice' (3–4), like the poet communicating the depth of Demeter's sorrow. These images of despair have unyielding, bitter sounds: 'winter', 'stone', 'flint', while the hard 'k' sounds of 'break' and 'lake' echo Demeter's 'broken heart' (4–6). This image of the heart, the centre of love, is lifeless; it has become detached from Demeter as she uses it like a stone to 'break the ice' (4). The attempt is fruitless: 'it skimmed, / flat, over the frozen lake' (5–6).

Men seem to be absent from this poem. They are certainly never mentioned. But the icy cold, the 'tough', 'hard' landscape, could be said to have something of the masculine about it. In the Greek myth it is Hades' theft and rape of Persephone that has divided mother from daughter, woman from woman, and been the catalyst for the death of fertility. In the first verses of the poem, Demeter cannot create; her choice of words is limited. Feeling is lost. As with most poems in this volume, Duffy seems to be saying that the female voice is constrained by a **patriarchal** cultural tradition and must be renewed to find its own voice.

This renewal comes in the third **tercet**, as Persephone appears in the distance, walking towards her mother: 'She came from a long, long way, / but I saw her at last' (7–8). This is a distance of time as well as place, for Demeter has endured the long winter months of

CONTEXT

In ancient Greece the Eleusinian mysteries were highly secretive annual initiation rites for the cult of Demeter and Persephone. Initiates believe they acquired divine powers in the afterlife. The mysteries themselves are based on the myths relating to Demeter and Hades' theft of Persephone.

CHECK THE NET

There are many depictions of Demeter and Persephone in Greek and Roman art. Visit **www.metmuseum.org** and search for a fragment of the Great Eleusinian Relief. This reconstructed marble relief shows Demeter and Persephone giving ears of wheat to the youth Triptolemos, so that men may learn how to cultivate the land. The original is in the National Archaeological Museum in Athens.

CHECK THE BOOK

In his introduction to *The Greek Myths* (1955) Robert Graves notes that the three phases of the moon, new, full and old, depict the maiden, the nymph and the crone, as well as spring, summer and winter.

separation. As her daughter enters the poem, she transforms it. She is natural and fertile, walking 'across the fields, / in bare feet, bringing all spring's flowers' (9–10). Hard sounds give way to soft **alliteration** to create images of breath and life: 'I swear / the air softened and warmed as she moved' (11–12). In the closing **couplet personification** is used to accentuate the return of fertility in the 'blue sky smiling' (13). The sky's 'shy mouth' is the shape of the new moon and signifies the goddess Persephone. She is the 'new moon' (14), the **symbol** in Greek mythology of the maiden, of youth and the spring. The poem therefore not only celebrates the return of Persephone to her mother and the renewal of life, but the chance to begin afresh, woman to woman.

The poem is a **sonnet**, or very near it. It is a love poem from Demeter to her daughter. The traditional form of fourteen lines including a **rhyming couplet** is adapted and written in four **tercets** without rhyme, but with a closing rhyming couplet. This form creates a structure for the poem, and follows the traditional movement of a sonnet. Demeter's sorrow is presented in the first two verses, and a change is ushered in with the entrance of her daughter in the third. This develops into a resolution in the fourth tercet, lifting the depression of the early verses to create joy, which is confirmed by the rhyming couplet at the end.

CHECK THE BOOK

It is worth comparing Hugo's novel *The Hunchback of Notre Dame* with the various film adaptations and Duffy's perspective in her poem 'Mrs Quasimodo'.

CONTEXT

There are parallels with 'Mrs Quasimodo' in Charles Perrault's fairy tale 'Beauty and the Beast'.

EXTENDED COMMENTARIES

TEXT 1 – MRS QUASIMODO

Mrs Quasimodo is the speaker of the poem and wife of the bell-ringer Quasimodo, the main character of Victor Hugo's 1831 novel *Notre-Dame de Paris* (*The Hunchbback of Notre Dame*). Like her husband, she is physically disabled. In the poem she describes how they met, married and achieved some small status as a married couple. As the marriage declines, Quasimodo's rejection of her and his infatuation with a beautiful gypsy girl leads Mrs Quasimodo to take revenge and destroy the bells.

In this **free verse** poem, Duffy looks at the outsider from a female perspective. Mrs Quasimodo is despised for her deformity, and we can assume she is the mirror image of her husband, except for her gender. She is 'the village runt, name-called, stunted, lame, hare-lipped; / but bearing up, despite it all, sweet-tempered' (4–5): the ugly but stoical girl who bears the cross of her difference with fortitude. In a monochrome Paris reminiscent of the 1939 film of the book, she keeps out of sight, 'my lumpy shadow / lurching on its jagged alley walls' (10–11). She is described in an unusual way as 'an ugly cliché' (6), as though she is an overused figure of speech, ill-fitting. By **objectifying** her, she is placed outside humanity and as such has no power in society. This is similar to the concept of 'the Other', used in **feminism** (as well as in issues relating to class, race or disability) to refer to the way in which women are set apart by men and their natures misunderstood. In this way they become stereotyped and can be more easily controlled. This identity, which has been thrust on Mrs Quasimodo, only serves to reinforce her separateness and give credence to what is considered normal. Anger, frustration and resentment at both her treatment and condition are allowed no outward expression, and, as we discover at the end of the poem, have their consequences. Her only solace is the 'generous bronze throats' of the bells (2). Her love of them allows her to step outside the boundaries of her delineated character, revealing a sensitive, intelligent side to her nature.

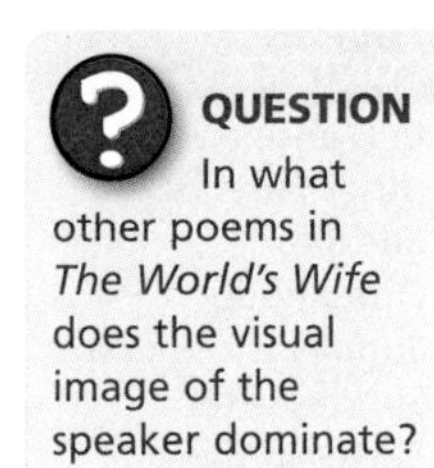

CONTEXT

Simone de Beauvoir (1908–86) first introduced the concept of 'the Other' in her essay 'Woman: Myth and Reality'. She commented that 'the Other' had an aura of mystery cast around it, and that this became a stereotype.

Living a strange life, high up in the great cathedral, she meets Quasimodo, someone with whom she feels she can identify. His lovemaking is rough and cruel. The image of the 'gaping, stricken bells' (31) witnessing her move from innocence to sexual experience implies foreboding; and the poignant words 'I wept' (32) suggest not only the cruelty of the lovemaking, but her gratefulness and relief at being wanted at all. Her need for love and acceptance is overwhelming and she places her trust in him. They marry, and her happiness is encapsulated in the epithalamium Quasimodo rings for her (34). He also rings an angelus (39), and this devotional peal, which in the Christian religion proclaims that Christ the Son of God is made human, **symbolises** Mrs Quasimodo's new state. Her marriage makes her almost human in the eyes of society. Though the Quasimodos are regarded as '*Gross*' (56), they nonetheless have 'got a life' (57) and have been granted some small crumb of normality. There are indications, however, that all is not well. Mrs Quasimodo says: 'And did I kiss / each part of him – / … or not?' (42–51). She has touched his deformities, but not his heart.

CONTEXT

An epithalamium is a poem or song celebrating marriage.

CONTEXT

In France and other parts of Europe, Quasimodo Sunday is the first Sunday after Easter in the Roman Catholic Church. The name comes from the Latin phrase 'Quasi modo geniti infantes' ('As newborn babes') which refers to the people baptised at Easter. In Victor Hugo's novel, Quasimodo was found abandoned on the steps of the cathedral on this day, hence his name.

CHECK THE BOOK

Berger's seminal book *Ways of Seeing* (1972), based on a BBC television series of the same name, draws attention to the viewer and the viewed. 'Men look at women. Women watch themselves being looked at' (p. 47). The book gives useful insights into how we might regard Mrs Quasimodo compared with the gypsy girl.

Mrs Quasimodo carries out her wifely duties in the cathedral grounds, in the company of 'gargoyles' and 'fallen angels' (58) – further examples of creatures expelled from humanity – until the marriage falters. Although written in **free verse**, the poem is punctuated every so often by a single line – 'So more fool me' (52); 'I should have known' (79) – which serves to steady the pace and allow Mrs Quasimodo to look back and reflect on the course of the marriage. As the marriage fails, Quasimodo's authoritarian nature is asserted; he not only withholds affection, but humiliates and rejects her. His cruelty is fuelled by his voyeuristic infatuation with a beautiful gypsy girl – the Esmeralda of Victor Hugo's novel.

Duffy, in exploring difference here, also explores other themes such as the male gaze, an idea famously discussed by the art critic, novelist and painter John Berger (b.1926) in his work *Ways of Seeing*. Men look at women, he says, in the assumption that they can do something to or for them; this gives them power. Women, on the other hand, are split; they view themselves being looked at and constantly carry their own image with them. This process is internalised and establishes the relationship not only between men and women, but also between women and themselves. In this context it is useful to consider Mrs Quasimodo's relation to herself and her husband and his to both her and Esmeralda. Mrs Quasimodo discovers that her husband in his infatuation is no different from other men. He is susceptible to the gypsy girl's beauty and wants to possess it; Mrs Quasimodo is punished by him for her lack of beauty. For Mrs Quasimodo, her husband's betrayal is more than she can bear. She had assumed commitment and a common identity where there was none. As she says: 'it's better, isn't it, to be well formed' (80) and 'beautiful' (83). Mrs Quasimodo equates beauty with goodness, as most of the world does. Her fragile self-esteem, her view of herself, collapses when she compares herself with the gypsy girl. Her self-hatred, voiced as the abuse that has been hurled at her over the years – '*Abortion. Cripple. Spastic. Mongol. Ape*' (103) – becomes self-destruction.

This is uncomfortable reading and leads to the final part of the poem, in which Mrs Quasimodo seeks revenge. The bells are no longer a comfort to her; instead they have been **personified** into lovely women who are Quasimodo's mistresses, 'Marie',

'Josephine' and others. They are **symbols** of everything that Mrs Quasimodo is not and is measured against. So in her grief she violently destroys each one. The tools she uses, 'my claw-hammer, / my pliers, my saw, my clamp' (111–12), are ungainly and vengeful extensions of herself as she wreaks havoc. This is as much an act of self-loathing as one of revenge. In making the bells 'mute' (121) she also silences herself: 'I wanted silence back' (136). The silence she yearns for is oblivion, a time before language, before identity is fully formed. In the last lines she acts out the **clichéd** role prescribed to her, debasing the bells she once loved and becoming the very thing she hates most: bestial and non-human, the monstrous outsider.

CHECK THE FILM

One of the most acclaimed adaptations of *The Hunchback of Notre Dame*, made in 1939, starred Charles Laughton as Quasimodo and was directed by William Dieterle. One of the most recent is a Disney animation (1996). This version is loosely based on Hugo's novel, and has an altered ending to suit modern sensibilities. A sequel followed in 2002.

GLOSSARY

23 **campanologists** bell-ringers

122 **arpeggios** when notes of chords are played in rapid succession

stretti a close series of overlapping statements

trills the rapid alternations of two tones

Text 2 – The Devil's Wife

In this poem 'the Devil's wife', Myra Hindley, narrates her involvement in a series of murders known as the Moors Murders, and her subsequent mental breakdown in prison. The murders were especially gruesome and have remained in the public imagination for over forty years. Children and one young man were the victims. The poem is divided into five parts: Hindley's sinister attraction to the Devil, Ian Brady; her involvement in the murders, and the trial and imprisonment; her sense of dislocation and denial; her religious belief and confessions of further crimes; and finally her appeal for parole.

Carol Ann Duffy attempts to explore this difficult subject by focusing on Myra Hindley. As a rule, the idea that women as well as men can commit sadistic crimes, particularly against children, is abhorrent to the public. Such acts by women are seen as particularly heinous and unnatural, because women are associated with protective mother love. As the speaker says: 'but I was the

CONTEXT

In 1966 Ian Brady and his accomplice Myra Hindley were convicted of the murders of Lesley Ann Downey, aged ten; and Edward Evans, aged seventeen. Ian Brady was further convicted of the murder of John Kilbride, aged twelve; and in 1986 Brady and Hindley confessed to two more murders: that of Keith Bennett, aged twelve; and Pauline Reade, aged sixteen.

CHECK THE NET

A BBC obituary of Hindley can be found at **http://news.bbc.co.uk**

CONTEXT

In 1997 a painting of Myra Hindley by Marcus Harvey was exhibited at the Royal Academy Sensation Exhibition in London. It was made up of children's handprints and caused considerable controversy.

Devil's wife / which made me worse' (part 2, 'Medusa', 14–15). Ian Brady, according to the judge, was beyond redemption, while Myra Hindley in his opinion could be reformed once separated from her lover's influence. It is she, however, who preoccupied the public and the media, and continues to do so even after her death.

The potency of Hindley herself as a visual image in the poem immediately works on the reader. The police mugshot of Hindley with her bleached blonde hair has become infamous. In many of the other poems in *The World's Wife* this identification with a visual image is less immediate because these figures are not in the public eye, as in the case of the wives of famous men, and must be conjured up in the reader's imagination. It is therefore the image of Myra Hindley rather than a wife of the Devil that dominates the poem. With this in mind, we need to remind ourselves that the poem is a work of imagination and not necessarily a true portrait of how Myra Hindley might have felt – this is not always easy to do, and is a mark of the poem's success.

Throughout the poem the Devil's wife is given various **personae**. This device allows the poet to investigate the character's changing motivations. In the first part, 'Dirt', she is an ordinary office clerk, who becomes a malignant force as the Devil enters her life, while in 'Medusa' she is the monstrous Gorgon. In part 4, 'Night', she is the lifer – the prisoner who will never gain freedom. Whatever her persona, she is similar to Mrs Quasimodo, an outsider, regarded as monstrous – Mrs Quasimodo because of her deformity, the Devil's wife because of her actions. Although the poem is too short for the individual parts to be regarded as **cantos**, it does have major divisions which allow Duffy to examine separate scenarios that make up the larger work. In 'Dirt' the speaker's attraction to the Devil is perverse. While the Devil is 'sarcastic and rude' (4), it is these very qualities that arouse her. She senses a common bond; some need or desire in her responds to him and she follows it. 'I gave / as good as I got till he asked me out' (7–8), she boasts, until he as the Devil violently possesses her both physically and spiritually and she becomes demonic: 'I swooned in my soul' (11). The act of burying 'a doll' (12) suggests the shocking image of a child being buried. Duffy avoids directly mentioning this, perhaps to convey the Devil's wife's inability to deal with the reality of what she has done – that she is in denial. In their predatory quest they remove themselves from normal society: 'We gave up going to work. It was either the woods / or looking at playgrounds, fairgrounds' (14–15). These highly disturbing images culminate in her fully fledged persona as the abuser and the abused. She is brutalised by the Devil's violence and ill-treatment of her: 'Two black slates / for eyes. Thumped wound of a mouth' (17–18). Under his influence she has lost all feeling and is silenced: 'I felt like this: Tongue of stone' (17). These abrupt images and the use of **caesura** accentuate the tone of this section. In the last words – 'Nobody's Mam' (18) – any links with maternal affection are severed, and they possess a harsh, resounding finality.

The subject of part 2, 'Medusa', is the trial, leading to conviction and imprisonment. The Devil's wife flies in her 'chains over the wood' (1), returning in her mind to the scene of one of the crimes, where a doll/child is buried. This is also a reference to the time when Hindley was taken to Saddleworth Moor by the police to identify the graves of the children. The Devil's wife recalls her part in the events, and the trial, in which she feels the forces of the law and the media are against her: 'Nobody liked my hair. Nobody liked how I spoke' (5). It also highlights her concern with trivia in the face of appalling crimes, and her sense of dislocation from the events of the trial, again accentuated by the use of caesura and short abrupt lines. She attempts to shift the responsibility for her part in the crimes to the Devil: 'He held my heart in his fist and he squeezed it dry' (6). When she faces the media she gives the cameras her 'Medusa stare' (7) and, like Medusa of Greek mythology, seems capable of turning anything to stone (see also the discussion of Duffy's poem 'Medusa' in **Detailed summaries**). Imprisonment confronts her, and she comes to realise that parole at some point in the future is unlikely, since she is 'the Devil's wife / which made me worse' (14–15).

While in prison Hindley underwent a religious reawakening. There were conflicting opinions regarding her beliefs: there were those who claimed she had become a reformed woman, and her religious belief was a manifestation of this; others viewed it as a ploy to gain a sympathetic hearing from the parole board. In part 3, 'Bible', written as a **sonnet**, Duffy presents the Devil's wife as a dislocated, disturbed woman repeatedly distancing herself from the crime in a

CONTEXT

The bodies of the children John Kilbride and Lesley Ann Downey and seventeen-year-old Edward Evans were found in 1965, soon after the murders. It was not until November 1986 that Hindley and Brady confessed to further murders, and were taken to Saddleworth Moor to search for the graves of Pauline Reade and Keith Bennett. Pauline Reade's body was discovered in July 1987; Keith Bennett's body has never been found.

CONTEXT

Hindley had converted to Roman Catholicism when she was fifteen after the death of a close friend, Michael Higgins, who was thirteen. Apparently she became obsessed by the loss.

CONTEXT

Lord Longford became a champion of Hindley soon after she was convicted. About twenty years after her conviction he attempted with a small group of supporters to gain her release, believing she had reformed. Others were not persuaded of this. All appeals for parole failed and she remained in prison. She died in November 2002.

chant-like voice that signals disintegration of the self, and therefore potential change. The **sonnet** is a controlled, ordered form usually associated with love poetry, and seems a strange choice here. But the sonnet is being used to restrain these disordered emotional thoughts. What seems to be the chaotic rambling of a disturbed woman is caught within the tightly controlled form, suggesting that there is method or purpose in her madness. Is she attempting to gain publicity in the hope that she will eventually be released? 'I said Send me a lawyer a vicar a priest. / Send me a TV crew send me a journalist' (5–6).

In the fourth part, 'Night', a short poem in the form of a prayer, which takes up the religious theme, it is suggested that after her fiftieth birthday, the 'fifty-year night', she will emerge from the darkness into the light of the morning and confess to further crimes. The section ends with the word 'Amen', meaning 'so be it', but may also be viewed **ironically** by those who see her as using religion for her own ends. The 'words that crawl out of the wall' (2) are those that have both haunted and hounded her throughout her imprisonment. Haunted because they emerge from her own mind; and hounded because they are words written as graffiti, by other prisoners, or have been used by the media and members of the public to denounce her.

The final part, 'Appeal', lists punishments the Devil's wife might have been subjected to in another time and place. They include torture and execution. The reiteration of 'If' (**anaphora**) contrasts these punishments with life imprisonment in line 10, so making connections with the national debate about the efficacy of the death penalty. At the end of the poem 'If' changes to 'But', signalling the final **couplet** in which the Devil's wife invites the reader to consider the effect her actions have had on her own life and the nation's, in other words privately and publicly. But the question is, does it also suggest reflection and remorse?

QUESTION

The couplet at the end of 'The Devil's Wife' asks a question. How would you answer it?

GLOSSARY

'Medusa' 10	**nowt** Yorkshire dialect meaning 'nothing'
'Appeal' 5	**peroxide** bleach used by Hindley to lighten her hair

TEXT 3 – EURYDICE

Eurydice, who has died, finds herself in the underworld and has no desire to be returned to life. She is aggrieved when her husband, the musician and poet Orpheus, follows in search of her. Her rejection of him is final, but whether she wants to or not she must return to the world and the life they had together. However, on the return journey she manages to escape by using flattery to outwit him. Duffy revises not only the myth, exploring gender roles, but also considers the nature of language.

In the traditional tale Eurydice is bitten by a serpent, dies and is taken to Hades, the place of the dead. Orpheus, the great musician and visionary of Greek mythology, who plays the lyre to magical effect, attempts to persuade the gods to return Eurydice to him. They agree on one condition: that throughout the journey to the upper world, he must walk ahead of Eurydice and not look back. He agrees. Unable to maintain his composure, he breaks the agreement and Eurydice is lost.

CONTEXT

In Greek mythology, Hades refers to both the underworld and the god of the underworld. Hades, along with Persephone, grants Orpheus his wish that Eurydice be returned to life.

Duffy's rewriting of the Greek myth is very different in spirit from the original. While she adheres to the plot and takes as her inspiration the figure of Eurydice, she imbues her with a fresh, modern **persona**, using, like all the poems in the collection, the **dramatic monologue** to do so. From the early lines, in which Eurydice addresses her female readers in a direct, sisterly fashion – 'Girls' (1) – we know she has something juicy to reveal. She arrives in Hades, the place of the dead. In ancient Greek the word means 'unseen'. In the poem, time – 'nowhen' (3) – as well as place has ceased to exist. The finality of death is present in the lines. It is emphasised by the use of **alliteration**, particularly the hard 'd' in 'dead' and 'down' (1), while the 'sh' sounds in 'shade' and 'shadow' (2–3) evoke the frail, insubstantial nature of Eurydice as a ghost. Language too has ceased, so that a full stop becomes the black hole of astronomical time and space.

CONTEXT

In astronomy a black hole is a region of space that has a gravitational field so strong that no matter can escape. The term is used informally to refer to a place where lost objects are thought to disappear, never to be seen again.

But in the last line of the first verse, the reader receives a surprise. Eurydice's arrival in the underworld has comes as a relief to her. It suits her perfectly, because it allows her to escape from her husband, Orpheus – and a clue to the nature of her discontent is presented to us. For Eurydice Hades is a place 'where words had to come to an end', whether 'famous or not' (6–9). Orpheus, with his poetry and 'words', is the problem. She recalls their time together, describing him in unflattering terms as a needy, self-obsessed man, sulky and oversensitive to criticism, who, if not exactly a stalker, has always relied too heavily on her. His preoccupation is his work and reputation in the literary world; her role has been to massage his ego and to reaffirm his status. In life he was always at her heels, and in death he cannot leave her alone, finally pursuing her to Hades, knocking 'at Death's door' (28), an image that **parodies** Bob Dylan's song 'Knockin' on Heaven's Door'. Indeed, the Orpheus of the poem is a **pastiche** of an ageing rock star and poet. For 'lyre' we could read 'guitar'. Eurydice disparagingly calls him the 'Big O' (30) with 'a poem to pitch' (33).

CONTEXT

Bob Dylan (b.1941), an American singer-songwriter, musician and poet, wrote 'Knockin' on Heaven's Door' for the film *Pat Garrett and Billy the Kid* (1973).

As she recounts their history together we learn how Orpheus was once 'Legendary' (36), and a great marketing success to boot. In the myth, Orpheus is able to charm the animals and birds with his voice and music; in the poem they become his adoring fans, from 'aardvark to zebra' (39) – if the advertising hype on the jacket cover of his books is to be believed. Eurydice has another more cynical tale to tell. As 'His Muse' (22), his typist and general dogsbody she knows better. If she could have her time again she would rather speak for herself than be placed on a pedestal as the 'Dark Lady' (49) and be mute. Like Little Red-Cap in Duffy's poem of that name, Eurydice is in search of her own poetic voice. And if she can't have it, she declares **ironically**, addressing the female reader confidentially again: 'girls, I'd rather be dead' (50). Though an ironic, **colloquial** line, it is also a dark comment.

CONTEXT

In Greek mythology the Muses are nine sister goddesses, daughters of Zeus and Mnemosyne. Each is responsible for a different art or science. The term 'muse' has come to refer to someone (usually a woman) who is the source of inspiration for an artist.

Orpheus has other ideas, however. He uses his music to manipulate the gods, who, 'like publishers', are 'usually male' (51–2). As Orpheus 'strutted his stuff' (55), the gods soften and pronounce that Eurydice must return to the upper world and Orpheus – without, of course, consulting her. By taking the myth and placing it in contemporary society the poet draws attention to several aspects of the cultural and economic world of the late twentieth century. The poem is clearly **feminist** in spirit, but it is also critical of a culture in which celebrity and fame are more important than what is said or written, where an artist's work becomes a bargaining tool or a 'deal' (54). For Eurydice this trap of returning to the world is critical. As part of the living, she will be confined to Orpheus' language, 'trapped' in his poetic techniques: 'images, metaphors, similes', his verse and poetic forms: 'octaves and sextets, quatrains and couplets, / elegies, limericks, villanelles', and the 'histories, myths' (63–6) he creates about her as his muse. Not only are they his words and not hers, but they are words dominated by the masculine perspective.

So on the journey back to the living world, Eurydice plots how to be free and tells us her version of the myth. Images of death abound, some comic, as she tries to plead with him to release her, until inspiration comes to her – rather than him. Knowing Orpheus well, she realises that flattery might make him stop and turn: '*Orpheus, your poem's a masterpiece. / I'd love to hear it again …*' (102–3). And she succeeds. In his conceit, he turns and destroys the thing he most wants. The last part of this **free verse** poem is written in three **tercets**, and appropriately the poem becomes more formal. The pace slows at the parting of Eurydice and Orpheus, and signals the end of the poem. The moment that Orpheus turns is depicted. It is an ordinary moment, not spectacular, mundane even. She notices that he hasn't shaved. Then she vanishes to find her own home in Hades, a place beyond language.

At a deeper level Duffy is discussing the nature of language in this poem. There is always a gap between what we want to say and what we actually say, especially for the poet, who struggles to capture the essential nature of an experience or idea through image and **metaphor**. The last tercet becomes a metaphor for this very point, and also takes us back to the beginning of the poem where Eurydice has arrived in Hades, the place where language ceases. 'The dead are so talented' (110) because they are silent. They have dispensed with words not because there is nothing to say, but because what can be said is never sufficient. Words are never fully able, however skilfully they are used by the artist, to express the essence of something. That essence is always a mystery, and will remain so. In their silence, the dead know this and are beyond words. They are wiser than the living, who can only 'walk by the edge of a vast lake' (111). The lake, like the central nature of experience, is deep, unfathomable. It remains uncontrolled, beyond manipulation by words, and will never yield up its secrets.

CHECK THE FILM

The Brazilian poet Vinicius de Moraes (1913–80) retold the story of Eurydice and Orpheus in his play *Orfeu da Conceição*, and the French director Marcel Camus later took this play and turned it into his classic film *Black Orpheus* (1959), setting it in the Brazil of the 1950s.

CONTEXT

In the Greek myth, when Orpheus dies he is reunited with Eurydice in Hades. In some interpretations this death is the beginning of a new life; in Duffy's poem Eurydice begins a new life without Orpheus.

CHECK THE NET

The story of Eurydice and Orpheus has strong links with the Japanese story of Izanami and Izanagi. Search Wikipedia – **www.wikipedia.org** – for more details of the Japanese legend.

GLOSSARY

15 **Eternal Repose** death

49 **Dark Lady** a reference to Shakespeare's possible inspiration for his **sonnets**

57 **Sisyphus** punished by Hades and made to roll a stone to the top of a hill for eternity

58 **Tantalus** in Greek mythology accused of presenting the gods with a sacrificial feast of human flesh and blood, and banished to the deepest part of Hades, his punishment to be for ever hungry and thirsty

PART THREE

CRITICAL APPROACHES

THEMES

THE FEMALE VOICE

In *The World's Wife* Carol Ann Duffy explores what it is to be a woman. In her efforts to do this, the poet is greatly assisted by her use of the **dramatic monologue**. The speakers are all female, and the audience is sometimes singled out as female too, for example in 'Eurydice': 'Girls, I was dead and down' (1), and 'Frau Freud': 'Ladies, for argument's sake' (1). This technique creates an immediate level of intimacy between speaker and reader, which in turn prepares the way for the expression of feminine intimacy in these poems. This is not to say that men's voices are never heard. Though they are always mediated through the female voice, we do hear their words in certain poems. We hear the words of Faust in 'Mrs Faust', for example, as he tells his wife that he has betrayed her, not with a real woman, but with '*a virtual Helen of Troy*' (93); and the words of the puritanical sex-changed Tiresias, who does not wish his wife to kiss him in public, are recorded. We also hear the words of Delilah's lover, the alpha male who seems troubled by his inability to be 'gentle, or loving, or tender' (19).

CHECK THE BOOK

Deryn Rees-Jones has written a clear and useful chapter on *The World's Wife* and Duffy's exploration of the female experience in *Consorting with Angels: Essays on Modern Women Poets* (2005).

Although the portrayal of men in the collection is not as a rule sympathetic, it is varied; and however unsympathetic it appears, it should be remembered that all the figures are **constructs**. In other words, they are figments of the writer's imagination, reworked in the reader's mind. Duffy's male figures are often a foil for the poet's humour, just as, at times, her female figures are. The depiction of the recipe for pig, a **metaphor** for the male chauvinist, is outrageously comic in 'Circe'. But so too is the double act of the Kray sisters, as they sentimentally recall their past and how, 'dressed to kill / and swaggering' (62–3), they 'leaned on Sinatra to sing for free' (64). While casting a witty and **ironic** eye on heterosexual relationships, in which women usually have the upper hand and the dominant voice, Duffy also explores the poignancy, anger and even horror involved in failed or dysfunctional relationships: for example the poignancy of Mrs Quasimodo's

CHECK THE BOOK

The Madwoman in the Attic: The Woman Writer and the Nineteenth-Century Literary Imagination (1979) by Sandra M. Gilbert and Susan Gubar looks at cultural and sexual stereotyping.

CHECK THE BOOK

Read Janet Montefiore's accessible article 'Feminism and the Poetic Tradition' in *Feminist Review*, 13 (spring 1983), in which she discusses women writers and their conflicting relationship with literary tradition. Montefiore looks at different approaches by women poets, including Adrienne Rich (b.1929).

CHECK THE BOOK

Cora Kaplan's *Salt and Bitter and Good: Three Centuries of English and American Women Poets* (1975) is a compilation of the work of women poets from the past, starting with Anne Bradstreet (c.1612–72) and concluding with Sylvia Plath (1932–63). It is accompanied by an excellent introduction and information on each poet.

rejection, the anger of Medusa's jealousy, and the horror of the relationship between the Devil and the Devil's wife.

Through the simultaneously imaginative and commonplace female voices she creates, Duffy explores not only what it is to be a woman, but also what it is to be a woman writing. As Cora Kaplan says in *Salt and Bitter and Good: Three Centuries of English and American Women Poets* (p. 13): 'Women's poetry vindicates women's experience not so much by praising it, as by questioning and exploring it'. Kaplan also notes that as she compiled these poems she came to be aware of 'how women poets fought to express a view of the world and the self that was singular to their sex but as comprehensive as any male perspective'.

Like Sylvia Plath, Duffy has spent much of her writing life exploring her own female writing identity. Plath's identity, however, was fraught with anxiety. Her attitude to both the feminine and the masculine was complicated by the loss of her father in childhood and an unsatisfactory relationship with her mother. Apart from her personal difficulties, the constrained culture of the post-war 1950s and early 1960s was not an easy one for the female poet who was also a wife and mother, and who wished to break away from the traditions of past women writers in her exploration of the female voice. In *The World's Wife* Duffy uses a particular combination to explore her writing identity: the **dramatic monologue** coupled with language from a wide variety of contexts. This combination has helped her articulate female experience through a multitude of female voices. In doing so she has reached a new and much wider audience that may continue to follow her further explorations of the feminine identity.

MARRIAGE

Marriage, a central theme in *The World's Wife*, is scrutinised through the eyes of the female speakers in a variety of contexts and from different perspectives. Many poems are told tongue-in-cheek at masculine expense, but there is always, with the exception of the very short poems 'Mrs Icarus' and 'Mrs Darwin', an attempt to explore the experience of women's lives. Duffy creates a sense of intimacy between speaker and reader through the dramatic monologue helped by the use of **colloquial** language. In some poems, particularly where colloquial language is used from the outset to express antagonism or contempt, the effect is startling. The reader immediately feels as if they have been invited to hear an exposé of the speaker's marriage. 'First things first – / I married Faust', announces Mrs Faust (1–2). 'That's him pushing the stone up the hill, the jerk', says Mrs Sisyphus (1); 'he could bore for Purgatory', complains Mrs Aesop (1). In other poems there is world-weariness rather than vexation. Mrs Rip Van Winkle has dragged herself towards an inert middle age, where she has sunk 'like a stone' (1). All these poems portray examples of the long-suffering wife. Mrs Sisyphus 'lie[s] alone in the dark' (25), her marriage marginalised by her husband's relentless, 'one hundred per cent' commitment to work (32). The whole poem echoes the word 'work' in both the rhyme endings and the jerky movement as Sisyphus pushes the stone – the burden of work – up the hill. In the case of Mrs Aesop, her husband's fables, constantly and ponderously told, 'slow as marriage' (14), have driven her not only to distraction but to viciousness, when she attacks his masculinity at the end of the poem.

QUESTION What does Mrs Sisyphus feel the loss of in her marriage?

Duffy does not hold back. These poems have a depth, a dark humour, as well as witty exuberance, and never more so perhaps than in 'Mrs Faust'. We are given the history of Mrs Faust's marriage: 'We met as students, / shacked up, split up, / made up, hitched up, / got a mortgage on a house' (3–6) and so on, until the marriage becomes merely a semblance of one. Finally it vanishes altogether as Faust disappears into the jaws of hell. Mrs Faust benefits from his demise; she secures her independence and inherits Faust's ill-gotten gains. Whether she deserves these or not is open to question; she shares Faust's greed, even if she is not complicit in his crimes. By contrast with Mrs Faust, Mrs Midas' response is different. Her complacent but not unhappy middle-class marriage is also shattered by her husband's greed, but she seems left in a state of limbo, angry at his selfishness but grieving for a marriage that has gone. There is a moving image at the end of 'Mrs Midas' when she 'think[s] of him in certain lights' (64) and experiences the loss of physical contact with him. Pity and love are bound together, and Duffy is like a wicked puppeteer pulling the strings.

Misfortune can fall on the good Mrs Midas while the not-so-good Mrs Faust can reap rewards.

Schisms exist in varying degrees between husband and wife throughout the volume. Mrs Lazarus, distraught at her husband's death, learns to adapt over time and find a new love, so that when Lazarus rises from his grave she is appalled. Pilate's wife expresses contempt for Pilate's inability to act with moral courage in his treatment of the Nazarene, and Frau Freud relishes the chance to upstage her husband and attack his theories. At times the reader might feel that for Duffy the relationships between men and women are impossible or doomed to fail, but there are some moments of joy. The sheer passion and eroticism of the lines spoken by Shakespeare's wife, Anne Hathaway, about her love for her husband, and his for her, is a delight:

> The bed we loved in was a spinning world
> of forests, castles, torchlight, clifftops, seas
> where he would dive for pearls. (1–3)

Although the **sonnet** pays homage to Shakespeare's poetry, it is also a celebration of a marriage. Perhaps the most moving image of the wife, however, is that of the outsider Mrs Quasimodo, which has a note of **tragedy**. When she feels a kindred spirit with Quasimodo, and through their union begins to take a place in society, she discovers that her commitment to him is misplaced. His obsession for the 'pin-up gypsy' (75) is more than betrayal. It confirms Mrs Quasimodo's fear that to be loved you must be beautiful, so that she is driven to 'an ecstasy of loathing' (94) and becomes not only alienated from the marriage but once again from society.

CONTEXT

Roland Barthes (1915–80) was an influential French philosopher, literary critic and **post-structuralist**. In *Mythologies,* his 1957 collection of essays, he looks at the powerful nature of ancient stories and the way in which they have come to affect our values and beliefs. This is what he means when he says that the myth 'transforms history into nature'.

The **motif** that runs through these marriages and the volume as a whole is the myth, the fairy tale, the **iconic** story or figure. It has often been observed that in ancient myths and tales, male characters are typically more powerful and dominant than females. Critics have suggested that the role of storytelling in our culture has been so strong over many centuries that these ancient stories have helped turn this imbalance into a reality, to the extent that the idea of men as dominant and women as submissive has become strongly embedded in our culture and we accept this hierarchy of gender as truth. In revisiting these iconic stories and figures, Duffy therefore challenges not only modern assumptions about marriage and gender roles, but also the very origins of these stereotypes. For further discussion see **The power of the tale** and **Revisionism**.

CHECK THE BOOK

In their introduction to *The Poetry of Carol Ann Duffy: 'Choosing Tough Words'* (2003), Angelica Michelis and Antony Rowland discuss how myth is often the site of gender conflict in its depiction of male and female identities (pp. 26–7).

SEXUALITY

If heterosexuality is largely rejected in *The World's Wife*, lesbian sexuality is affirmed. Meaningful relationships tend, with the exception of 'Anne Hathaway', to be found in communities of women. '*Elvis is alive and she's female*' is the rallying cry at the beginning of 'Elvis's Twin Sister'. The sister in question, a nun, leads a contented life. There is a complete absence of conflict in the poem. There is only, in the last verse, a remembrance of past sorrow from a previous life as – we can assume – Elvis. Reborn as Sister Presley, she receives the Reverend Mother's appreciative gaze, who 'digs the way I move my hips / just like my brother' (9–10). Although lesbianism is not explicitly explored in the volume, it is given positive treatment where it occurs. The black Queen in 'Queen Herod' is a self-assured, imposing figure, who stares at Queen Herod 'with insolent lust' (30).

CHECK THE BOOK

Jeffrey Wainwright looks at different sexual **personae** in '*from* Mrs Tiresias' in 'Female metamorphoses: Carol Ann Duffy's Ovid' (pp. 48– 50) in *The Poetry of Carol Ann Duffy: 'Choosing Tough Words'*, edited by Angelica Michelis and Antony Rowland (2003).

Mrs Tiresias undergoes a life-changing experience as well as her husband. Having struggled to help him cope with his unwanted sex change and experienced the deterioration and end of the marriage, she finds a new life. She takes a woman as a lover, and their relationship is depicted in loving and erotic terms. She describes 'her violet eyes', 'the blaze of her skin' and 'the slow caress of her hand on the back of my neck' (82–4). This relationship seems far more profound than the tedious marriage she has left behind. Tiresias is not so lucky in his new life, in which there is no sexual pleasure or delight. His female gender, forced upon him, does not sit comfortably. Although he is seen out and about as a woman in the company of 'powerful men' (62), his voice gives his residual masculinity away. Duffy creates a wonderfully original and apt image here to display its jarring femininity: 'A cling peach slithering out from its tin' (74). 'The Kray Sisters' is lavish in its depiction of the two women, who are brash, strident and noisy in the **feminist** cause. Although lesbianism is not specifically depicted, it exists in the reference to the numerous gay icons mentioned in the poem: 'Lulu, Dusty and Yoko' (56), among others. It is also present in the sisters' comic disapproval of those girls in the firm

CHECK THE FILM

The acclaimed play *Steaming* by Nell Dunn (b.1936), first performed at the Theatre Royal in London in 1981 and published in the same year, depicts a group of five women who come together in a Turkish bath, where they share their stories, hopes and desires. The play was made into a film starring Vanessa Redgrave and Diana Dors, and directed by Joseph Losey. It was released in 1985, a year after Losey's death in 1984.

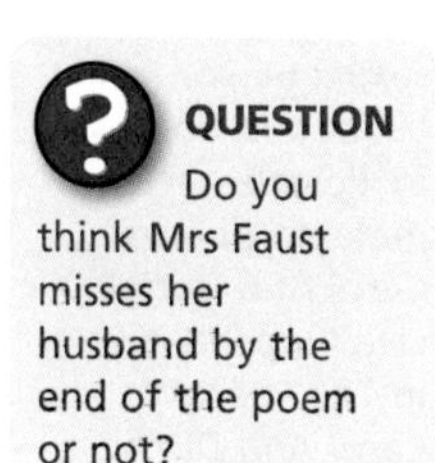

QUESTION

Do you think Mrs Faust misses her husband by the end of the poem or not?

who, 'well out of order', get 'Engaged' or become 'some plonker's wife' (40–2) 'up the Mile End Road'. Duffy portrays communities of women from different angles and she is not afraid to be irreverent about them.

There are other kinds of sexuality that Duffy explores in the rejection of marriage. Some female speakers choose to be single, which is itself an act of empowerment. Eurydice and Pygmalion's bride use their wits to escape their marriages, and Penelope finds fulfilment elsewhere, in creative power. Mrs Rip Van Winkle blossoms while her husband slumbers, literally finding a whole new world through travel and through her love of the arts, but her good fortune is curtailed when he wakes. Mrs Faust also pursues the single life, and for periods lives separately from Faust. Division early in the relationship followed by reconciliation is recorded in quick-fire succession in the opening verse. By verse nine, when the marriage has all but collapsed, Mrs Faust goes her 'own sweet way' (74). But, significantly, she returns. Though she is brittle, acquisitive and superficially independent, the reader is never quite convinced that Faust relinquishes his hold on her. To what extent this is a sexual hold we are not sure. But Mrs Faust seems to be drawn to those who transgress. When Mephistopheles pays a visit, she notes: 'I smelled cigar smoke, / hellish, oddly sexy, not allowed' (42–3). We can also speculate that staying wealthily married is cynical greed on her part; but it could also be that she feels a genuine affinity with Faust, however unfeeling he has become, and she remains loyal to his memory: 'I keep Faust's secret still' (133).

Other speakers, most obviously Mrs Beast, treat their heterosexual relationships with complete – albeit comic – cynicism. She chooses a heterosexual relationship in which she can be an alpha female, overwhelmingly dominant, and advises all women to do so. By choosing this course she turns the usual assumption about male dominance and female passivity on its head. Her time is spent in the company of women like herself, all married to outsiders who are presumably like the Beast, both subservient and grateful. Mrs Beast acts out her role as the stereotypical, insensitive, violent male, who makes the Beast suffer when she is troubled: 'So I was hard on the Beast, win or lose, / when I got upstairs' (81–2).

If 'Mrs Beast' is darkly comic, Duffy is not afraid to explore sexual violence in its more horrific manifestations. It is largely present in the heterosexual relationships, but it is not necessarily perpetrated by men, though examples are included. In 'The Devil's Wife' the Devil is sexually abusive towards his wife, as well as being a violent child murderer. Quasimodo is brutal to Mrs Quasimodo as well being brutalised. However, neither of these male figures is sufficiently developed to leave behind the kind of impression in the reader's mind that Salome does. She is ice-cold and calculating. The absence of feeling marks her out as a serial killer and makes the events described all the more disturbing. The images are often horrifying. The 'beautiful crimson mouth' (10) of the lover is not beautiful at all, but red with blood and 'Colder than pewter' (13). That Duffy manages to explore such a difficult area and carry it off with aplomb is testimony to her skill as a poet.

CONTEXT

Hérodiade, the 1884 opera by Jules Massenet (1842–1912), gives a quite different picture of Salome and her relationship with John the Baptist. She is not responsible for his death, and is presented as a committed and loving disciple.

MOTHERHOOD

Positive relations between women are also expressed through motherhood. Birth often acts as a transforming power. In 'Thetis' the sea nymph is pursued by her persistent and unwelcome suitor. The poem reads like a desperate chase as Thetis transforms herself into different forms – bird, snake, fish, mermaid and many others – in an effort to escape. Transforming her physical self is part of her nature and her power, but her pursuer is determined to seize her. She can never transform herself sufficiently to fully escape. When she succumbs to him, the final **transformation** is the birth of a child. What motherhood means to Thetis beyond transformation itself, we are not told. But the conviction in the words – she is 'turned inside out' (47) – declares this to be a more profound transformation than she has hitherto known.

In 'Pope Joan' there is also transformation and revelation. Duffy imagines a woman, Pope Joan, as the head of the Roman Catholic Church. In her role, one that can in reality only be held by a man, she changes unleavened bread into the **symbolic** body of Christ. The poem moves through her loss of faith towards the final verses, where she undergoes her own transformation, a 'miracle' (29), the birth of a child. As with Thetis, the experience of motherhood is profound. It is a confirmation of her female self.

Irish poet Eavan Boland's *An Origin Like Water: Collected Poems 1967–1987* (1996) includes the poem 'Child of Our Time', which explores motherhood and the death of a child in a Dublin bombing. Boland (b.1944) creates images from stories and lullabies.

There are also those in the volume, such as Mrs Faust, who choose not to be mothers. Generally there is no mention of daughters or sons unless motherhood is integral to the poem. In 'Mrs Faust' it is stated explicitly: she says that she and Faust 'flourished academically, / BA. MA. Ph.D. No kids' (7–8). Why is uncertain; Duffy must feel that this is a necessary character trait of Mrs Faust. The implication is that she is too busy acquiring status and wealth to become a mother. Or perhaps she is too unsympathetic to care for a child. But we are given no real clues. Mrs Faust could as well be given children as a fashionable acquisition. Since there are positive images in the collection of women who are not mothers – Sister Presley in 'Elvis's Twin Sister' is one – we can assume therefore that the poet is not saying that motherhood is a necessity for a woman's fulfilment. Perhaps she is saying that Mrs Faust is simply denying herself this joy.

The focus on motherhood in 'Queen Herod' is one of a fierce protection, as fierce as any wild animal and as violent. This is not the aspect of motherhood presented to us in 'Thetis' or 'Pope Joan'. Queen Herod, in the company of the three matriarchal Queens, 'those vivid three' (14), exists at a time when matriarchal power is threatened by the coming of masculine power, a 'bitter dawn' (15) **symbolised** by the birth of Jesus. Queen Herod is prepared to carry out the most violent of acts, and orders the killing of '*each mother's son*' (76) in an unmistakable reference to the Massacre of the Innocents. Prepared to go to extreme lengths to protect her daughter from men, she tells us: 'We wade through blood / for our sleeping girls. / We have daggers for eyes' (93–5).

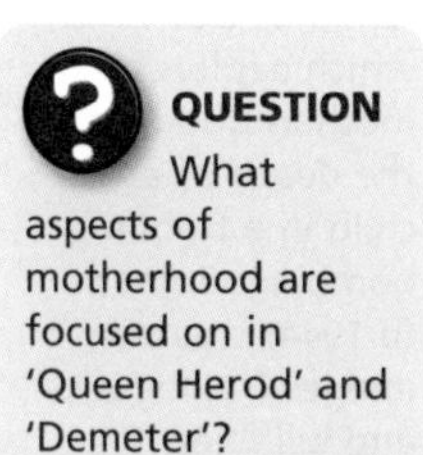

QUESTION What aspects of motherhood are focused on in 'Queen Herod' and 'Demeter'?

There are few poems in the volume that match the simplicity and optimism of 'Demeter' in its praise of motherhood. The transforming power that her daughter, Persephone in the Greek myth, brings with her as she returns from the underworld is for all humankind, not just for Demeter, who has existed in a wilderness during her daughter's absence. She brings renewal and new growth to the natural world. In this respect her daughter is the symbol of **transformation**. Avril Horner suggests that there is an 'emotional redemption' for Demeter in the poem. By this she means that Demeter is restored and healed by her daughter. She says: 'Duffy inverts the Greek myth so that, rather than the mother seeking to rescue the daughter from Pluto's cold clutches, it is the daughter who rescues the mother and who heals her broken heart'.

We could also add that the poem's placing – 'Demeter' is the last in the book – is redemptive in relation to the volume as a whole. The principal concern in the collection has been to explore the complex power relations between men and women and also highlight the dominance of Western masculine thought in **iconic** tales, in history and, by implication, in our value structures. Here the relationship between Demeter and her daughter not only emphasises the relations between women as empowerment, and a way forward in finding a **feminine** identity, but also celebrates the mother-daughter bond and the self-affirming nature of motherhood.

CHECK THE BOOK

These quotes can be found on pp. 116–17 of Horner's essay '"Small Female Skull": patriarchy and philosophy in the poetry of Carol Ann Duffy' in *The Poetry of Carol Ann Duffy: 'Choosing Tough Words'*, edited by Angelica Michelis and Antony Rowland (2003). Horner's essay offers an accessible and enlightening perspective on Demeter and the community of women.

POETIC FORMS

Carol Ann Duffy likes to use a variety of traditional poetic forms or versions of them. The expression of thoughts and feelings which are often disordered is not easy to accommodate within the regularity and order of traditional forms, and this creates challenges for the poet. When a poem is successful, however, the form itself helps to capture the essence of those thoughts and feelings. Duffy's **discourse** challenges the normal assumptions about women and therefore the status quo. In her poems, this radicalism is set against the traditional forms she calls on, such as the **dramatic monologue** and the **sonnet**, which have established conventions and are by their nature conservative. Perhaps it is the very tension between the two that Duffy enjoys.

In *The World's Wife* Duffy includes examples of the sonnet. She also uses a variety of verse structures, such as the **couplet**, the **tercet**, the **quatrain** and thc **sestet**. Many of the poems are written in **free verse** (*vers libre*), but all these exist within the dramatic monologue. She chooses this form for the female speaker of each poem, and although we hear men's words from time to time, they are always mediated through the female voice (see **Themes: The female voice**).

CHECK THE BOOK

Terry Eagleton in *Literary Theory: An Introduction* (1983, revised 1996) discusses the tension between discourse and form in literature, linking it to the work of the French **feminist** Julia Kristeva (b.1941) and her work in psychoanalysis (see pp. 187–93).

CONTEXT

The monologue should not be confused with the **soliloquy**. Hamlet's famous soliloquy 'To be, or not to be' is addressed to himself, even though the audience is listening.

CONTEXT

Robert Browning wrote several dramatic monologues. 'My Last Duchess' (1842) is his best-known example.

CONTEXT

Christina Rossetti's 'The Convent Threshold' (written around 1860) was inspired by the true story of the twelfth-century lovers Abelard and Heloise.

CHECK THE NET

To read 'The Convent Threshold' in its entirety, go to **www.victorianweb.org**

THE DRAMATIC MONOLOGUE

The monologue, in which a character addresses an audience, has a long theatrical history. Opera uses monologue too, and it is used in poetry, by the poet John Milton, for example. The **dramatic monologue**, which was popular in the Victorian period, is a development of this form. Robert Browning (1812–89) was its main practitioner. In his best work there is complex **imagery** and the character is fully developed. A dramatic monologue less often referred to is 'The Convent Threshold', written by Christina Rossetti (1830–94). A short examination of it illustrates the features of the dramatic monologue as conceived during the Victorian period. 'The Convent Threshold' is typically a **lyric** poem, written at length in which an imaginary female speaker, not the poet, is addressing her lover. We hear only her words, never his. Both have reached a critical point in their lives, again a feature of the form. She wishes to enter the convent because their love has caused family conflict: 'There's blood between us, love, my love, / There's father's blood, there's brother's blood', and by removing herself from the world and entering a convent, she can pay penance: 'And blood's a bar I cannot pass'. She pleads with him to repent as well, in order that they be reunited in Paradise: 'There we shall meet as once we met, / And love with old familiar love'. The use of speech allows the poet to shift the voice from the self (which seems like the poet's voice) and encourage the development of the speaking character. This technique can more easily create the sense that an argument is being presented – as here where the speaker is making the case for redemption. By allowing an imagined character to present his or her view in this way, we can see why Duffy finds the dramatic monologue so appealing. In particular it **foregrounds** the speaker-character and accommodates a combative style, both distinct features of *The World's Wife*.

Duffy is, of course, positioned quite differently from Christina Rossetti. Their concerns are not the same. In 'The Convent Threshold' the female speaker wishes to be reunited with her lover in a pure union after death. The speakers of *The World's Wife* have scant regard for men's souls. Both Duffy and Rossetti do, however, make it their business to give women a voice, to describe experience from a woman's perspective.

Carol Ann Duffy takes the dramatic monologue and makes the form her own, shaping it to her needs. Her poems can be lengthy diatribes or short and pithy exclamations like 'Mrs Icarus'. Ideal for performance, some are like the monologues of a stand-up comedian. The voices are theatrical and almost without exception fearless, a trait usually associated with masculinity. Delilah emasculates her lover by eliminating the source of his strength: 'Then with deliberate, passionate hands / I cut every lock of his hair' (41–2).

CHECK THE BOOK

Deryn Rees-Jones examines Duffy's use of the dramatic monologue in *Carol Ann Duffy* (2001), pp. 17–29.

THE SONNET

The word 'sonnet' comes from the mid sixteenth-century Italian *sonetto* meaning 'little sound' or 'song'. The traditional form, in which a single idea is set out and explored, and a conclusion arrived at, often by employing **conceits**, is complex. The final **couplet** sums things up or gives an additional twist to the conclusion. Traditional **sonnets** consist of fourteen lines and are written in **iambic pentameter**, and are either **Shakespearean** or **Petrarchan** (sometimes called Italian). They are usually love poems with a philosophical bent, though Shakespeare also included erotic themes in his sonnets, and subsequently other poets also introduced religious themes. The Shakespearean sonnet has an *abab cdcd efef gg* rhyme scheme; the Petrarchan is normally *abba abba* followed by a **sestet** *cdcdcd* or other rhyme patterns. John Donne (1572–1631), John Milton (1608–74) and William Wordsworth (1770–1850) have all written sonnets; much later W. H. Auden (1907–73) composed poetry in the sonnet form. He, like Duffy, enjoyed writing within a range of forms and probably influenced her. The sonnet is one of the most durable of all the poetic forms and is still popular with poets today, although modern poets often take the form and play with it to suit their own purposes. They usually abandon the rhyme and **metre**, but keep the fourteen lines with the end couplet, and also the spirit of the sonnet form.

CHECK THE NET

Further information about the **sonnet** can be found at **www.sonnets.org**

In *The World's Wife* there are four sonnets. The most easily recognisable is 'Anne Hathaway'. The remaining three are 'Bible', in 'The Devil's Wife'; 'Frau Freud'; and 'Demeter'. In 'Anne Hathaway' the theme of the poem, love, is ideal for a sonnet. Indeed, Duffy could hardly have chosen another form, since it celebrates the relationship between Shakespeare – whose collection

CHECK THE BOOK

W. H. Auden's sonnet 'Luther' stays within the traditional metre and, largely, the rhyme scheme. It is included in his *Collected Shorter Poems 1927–1957.*

CONTEXT

We do not know for whom Shakespeare wrote his sonnets. It is assumed, however, that they were not written for or about his wife (with the possible exception of Sonnet 145). A certain **irony** therefore accompanies the reading of 'Anne Hathaway'.

CONTEXT

Walt Whitman (1819–92) is considered to be America's greatest poet. His poetry is contained in *Leaves of Grass*, a lifetime's project.

CONTEXT

Christopher Smart (1722–71) is still popular today and his poems are often included in anthologies for schools. *Jubilate Agno* (1939) includes the poem 'My Cat, Jeoffrey', which can be found in *The Rattle Bag*, edited by Seamus Heaney and Ted Hughes (1982).

of **sonnets** contains some of the greatest love poems – and his wife. Set out in the same way as the typical **Shakespearean sonnet**, she also includes the **rhyming couplet** at the end.

The sonnet form used in 'Demeter' is looser. Written in four **tercets** and a final rhyming couplet, it again celebrates love, this time between a mother and her daughter. In contrast, 'The Devil's Wife' is the most disturbing poem in the volume. The speaker is the Moors Murderer Myra Hindley, cast as the wife, the Devil being Ian Brady. In part 3, 'Bible', Hindley, disturbed and paranoid, seems to be in denial, unable to admit her guilt: 'No not me I didn't I couldn't I wouldn't' (1), and shifts the blame to her accomplice: 'it was him it was him' (12). At first the subject seems a surprising choice for a sonnet. The relationship between Hindley and Brady involved sexual obsession; but sexual love, albeit tainted and abusive, is also a theme in the poem, so the form may be more in keeping than we might suppose.

FREE VERSE

Free verse (*vers libre*), is not to be confused with **blank verse**. The term suggests that there are no rules when writing in this form; and perhaps that there is no form at all. But free verse does have form, and rhythm too. While it does not follow the regular patterning of **metred** verse and traditional forms, it usually has some organising features, if only that it is written in lines.

Free verse as a movement supposedly began in the nineteenth century in France, but the American poet Walt Whitman, who wrote in what is considered free verse, possibly did more than any other poet to develop it. This lack of boundaries in form links to his ideas on democracy and personal freedom. Earlier in the eighteenth century the English poet Christopher Smart wrote in irregular rhythm in a style similar to biblical translations and which could be described as a type of idiosyncratic free verse. Occasionally free verse can be very close to prose in form. Carolyn Forché's stark poem 'The Colonel' is one such poem.

Free verse allows the individual poet to decide how to organise the work. Lines may have a full stop in the middle or run on into the next. A line can be any length, one word even. Duffy concludes the fourth part of 'The Devil's Wife' with 'Amen', while the line 'I showed no scratch, no scrape, no scar' from 'Pygmalion's Bride' (33) illustrates the use of **alliteration** and repetition, giving the poem regularity. T. S. Eliot is reputed to have claimed that no verse could be entirely free if it was to be successful. Duffy also introduces rhyme. Indeed, much verse that describes itself as free verse also contains rhyme, apparent or hidden. For an example from *The World's Wife*, see lines 78–82 of 'Queen Herod', which has a strong affinity with T. S. Eliot's 'The Journey of the Magi' (1927). The techniques demonstrated here all help to give free verse **cadence** and shape.

CONTEXT

Carolyn Forché (b.1950) is an American poet and human rights activist. In her free verse poem 'The Colonel', the colonel of the title empties a sack of dried human ears on the table in front of the **narrator**.

CONTEXT

Free verse, a translation of the French term *vers libre*, is also associated with such poets as Arthur Rimbaud (1854–91) and Jules Laforgue (1860–87), and later Ezra Pound (1885–1972) and T. S. Eliot (1888–1965).

LANGUAGE AND STYLE

One of Carol Ann Duffy's most distinctive features is the range and variety of her language. This, coupled with the strength of the female speakers as they shift in tone, while always remaining **foregrounded**, makes *The World's Wife* a striking collection. The female speakers are depicted in many different circumstances, and Duffy draws on the natural idioms of ordinary speech, slang, **cliché** and even profanity, while also creating **metaphors** that are rich and subtle. Her style can therefore include the bawdy, the **lyrical**, the disturbing and the tragic, and since Duffy's task is to reach a wide audience yet still create original images, her language is rarely inaccessible. She has commented: 'I like to use simple words but in a complicated way' (as recalled in an interview with Peter Forbes entitled 'Winning Lines', published in the *Guardian* on 31 August 2002). She also draws on different **registers** and recreates them in a way that strikes the reader as authentic. This is most obvious in poems such as 'The Kray Sisters', where the poet plays with the accent of the East London gangster of the 1960s, and in the language used to create the soft southern drawl in 'Elvis's Twin Sister'. Duffy is also interested in the nature of language itself, and in some of her volumes she explores this. Though this is not the main focus of *The World's Wife*, a fascination with language still

In his excellent and thoughtful essay '"What it is like in words": translation, reflection and refraction in the poetry of Carol Ann Duffy', Michael Woods examines Duffy's preoccupation with language and meaning. See *The Poetry of Carol Ann Duffy: 'Choosing Tough Words'*, edited by Angelica Michelis and Antony Rowland (2003).

To find out more about any of Duffy's fellow poets, visit **www.contemporary writers.com**; this site contains many up-to-date profiles.

exists. The sheer pleasure that Shakespeare's language gives, for example, is expressed in 'Anne Hathaway' in the exultant portrayal of the couple's lovemaking: 'his touch / a verb dancing in the centre of a noun' (6–7).

The female writing identity and its relationship to language is also explored. Eurydice is trapped by the masculine language of her husband, the poet and musician Orpheus: 'trapped in his images, metaphors, similes, / octaves and sextets, quatrains and couplets' (63–4) and so on until she uses it to trick him and thereby becomes empowered. In a vigorous image in the opening poem of the collection, Little Red-Cap takes 'an axe / to a willow to see how it wept' (36–7) because she is tired of the 'same old song' and the 'same rhyme, same reason' (35–6). In her struggle to use language afresh and to forge her own voice, Little Red-Cap echoes Duffy's struggle as a poet to forge originality out of words. There is a similar pattern in the poem 'Penelope', where the heroine embroiders her own history. Although there is no explicit reference to the features of language as there is in 'Little Red-Cap', the poem is a **metaphor** for Penelope's creative drive, mirroring the idea of the female writer fulfilling her purpose.

DARK HUMOUR AND DOUBLE MEANINGS

There is much wit and playfulness in *The World's Wife*, as well as dark humour, and Duffy uses many literary devices to create mood. Sometimes one device follows on the heels of another as she creates a series of images. In the following example from 'Circe' she deftly uses **alliteration** and **pun** together:

> Remember the skills of the tongue –
> to lick, to lap, to loosen, lubricate, to lie
> in the soft pouch of the face – (15–17)

The alliterative 'l' accentuates the erotic nature of the tongue, but the 'lie' has a **double meaning**. The tongue can 'lie' – tell untruths – as well as 'lie', rest benignly in the mouth. The success of these lines is also due to well-judged pacing. Duffy knows when to pause or to run on into the next line. The effect of the two dashes or pauses means lines 16 and 17 are emphasised. It becomes a cautionary aside to the reader, who can enjoy the lush 'l' sound before the impact of the pun 'lie', whose second meaning runs into the next line and the next pause.

In 'The Kray Sisters' there are also double meanings that are extended to create a spider's web of references. The imaginary 'Cannonball Vi' for example (18), the Kray sisters' **feminist** and pugnacious grandmother, has numerous connections to members of the real-life Kray family, including their boxing grandfather, and also to the suffragette Emily Davison. Double meanings are frequently hidden meanings, and the use of cockney rhyming slang, for example 'God Forbids' (kids), accentuates the Kray sisters' dubious underworld activities.

Words can also be used to give lines form as well as humour: 'One week ... / Two doctors ... / Three painkillers four times a day' (44–6), Mrs Tiresias announces when her husband is unable to cope with menstruation. Sometimes Duffy fires an insult as a sudden shock tactic to create surprise and amusement and to emphasise the point being made. This occurs twice in 'Mrs Aesop', at the end of a line, to convey the wife's exasperation. The element of surprise can also be used to much darker effect and to shift the mood dramatically. The casual, sardonic tone adopted throughout 'Salome' as the speaker tells us of her hedonist life is only punctured at the very end, when the mood shifts to one of horror and her true character is revealed. Duffy also uses **parody** by taking a character or setting and placing it in a different absurd context, in the case of the torpid Rip Van Winkle, for example.

SATIRE AND IRONY

Critics and reviewers have frequently described *The World's Wife* as witty, **ironical** and **satirical**. The volume as a whole can be described as a satire, since Duffy seeks to reveal the dynamics between men and women, in which women have historically had less power. The function of satire is to criticise human folly, affectation or corruption, by using wit, mockery and sometimes irony. Satire may target social attitudes, an institution or an individual (often someone in the public eye such as a celebrity or

CONTEXT

Hipponax of Ephesus was an ancient Greek poet living around 540BC who used satire and irony to attack his enemies and is recorded as being particularly cruel. He wrote **iambic** poetry and is considered to be the inventor of parody.

CONTEXT

During the seventeenth and eighteenth centuries there were several notable poets writing satire, including John Dryden (1631–1700) and Alexander Pope (1688–1744). Jonathan Swift (1667–1745), the author of *Gulliver's Travels* (1726), is also remembered as one of the foremost satirists.

CONTEXT

The word 'satire' is derived from the Latin *satira*, meaning 'a plate of colourful mixed fruits' or 'medley'. This definition could be used to describe *The World's Wife*.

CHECK THE BOOK

Duffy's poem 'Translating the English, 1989', published in her 1990 collection *The Other Country*, is a clever social satire.

politician) and it can be merciless in its criticism. **Satire** is by nature subversive and, however witty, it is used to make a serious point.

Though *The World's Wife* as a whole is satirical, not all the individual poems are. Several are celebratory, such as 'Demeter'. There is **pathos** in 'Mrs Quasimodo', 'Salome' shifts in tone to become shocking, and 'The Devil's Wife' is profoundly disturbing from beginning to end. But an example of a short satirical barb is the poem 'Mrs Darwin'. In a few lines, Duffy manages to debunk one of the greatest thinkers of the modern age. She does this not by decrying Darwin's theories, but by suggesting that his wife is the author of the idea that humans evolved from apes, while simultaneously insulting his ape-like features. In 'Mrs Sisyphus' the modern obsession with work and the male need for success is satirised, as is the male chauvinist in 'Circe'. Another satire is 'Mrs Faust'. This is evident not so much in the relationship between husband and wife but in the mockery of their lifestyle: from their desperate scramble up the social ladder – 'Fast cars' (12), 'dinner parties' (29) – to the dizzy heights, in Faust's case, of moon-walking. Mrs Faust, in the meantime, is sidelined, though eventually Faust is dragged away to hell. There is a supreme example of double **irony** in the poem. The mistreated Mrs Faust inherits all the wealth, while Faust, with no soul to sell, outwits even Mephistopheles.

There are many kinds of irony in literature and in life. But there is always an incongruity or discordance between what is *assumed* to be the case and what *is* the case – or what actually happens or is said. We can read irony in 'Delilah'. To become tender and caring Delilah's lover has to lose his masculine strength, so Delilah cuts off his hair; and yet his masculine strength is the very thing that distinguishes him as a man. In 'Pygmalion's Bride' there is irony too. Pygmalion's desire is to turn the female speaker from a statue to a woman, to feel her flesh and possess her: 'he squeezed, he pressed. / I would not bruise' (27–8). But when she responds in a full-blooded human way, expressing need, he does not want her. She, of course, is fully aware of what the outcome will be even if Pygmalion is not, since she engineers it as a means of escaping his unwelcome attentions. The female speaker's knowingness is not surprising. Irony is often the humour of the silenced or marginalised. It is a way of showing that they are only too aware of the reality of their social position and the forces against them.

IMAGERY

Imagery constructs not only the visual in the reader's mind, but all the associated feelings, actions, sounds and other sensual experiences. **Metaphor** and **simile** are often the vehicle for this. In certain poetry **figurative** language can be abstract and complex, intentionally so, but this is not generally the case in *The World's Wife*. Sometimes Duffy creates images that are startling and immediate, and at the beginning of certain poems they have the clear sharp language reminiscent of the imagist poets: 'Ice in the trees' is the opening image of 'Queen Herod'. But the diversity of the language and the references alluded to produce all manner of images. By contrast, almost the entire first verse of 'Little Red-Cap' is a series of images that create a solemn and portentous metaphor for burgeoning womanhood, beginning: 'At childhood's end, the houses petered out' and ending: 'till you came at last to the edge of the woods' (1–5). **Alliteration**, using 'b' and 's', helps to produce the rotting image of Medusa: 'My bride's breath soured, stank' (6). The 'honeyed embrace' (41) that would usually evoke **connotations** of sweetness and nourishment is a sinister golden trap for Mrs Midas, since everything her husband touches turns to gold. Some images are self-referential: in other words, Duffy refers to the **intertextuality** of the volume. At the beginning of 'Mrs Beast', myth, legend and fairy tale are evoked; Eurydice imagines herself trapped in Orpheus' 'histories, myths …' (66); while for Circe, the ships sail 'like myths' (33).

'Circe' has many lavish images. The succulent recipe for 'pig', a metaphor for men, is created with rich images of taste and smell, for example 'the bristling, salty skin' (4), along with sexual **allusion**: 'sweetmeats' (28). One of the most memorable images is a simile found in the first verse: 'the moon / like a lemon popped in the mouth of the sky' (9–10). It links to a memory; Circe recalls herself standing at dusk 'tasting the sweaty, spicy air' (9) as she stares at the heavens. The whole effect suggests Circe's romantic nature, before her disillusionment with men, as well as the image of the hog's head prepared as a dish. And at the very end of the poem,

CONTEXT

Imagism was a school of Anglo-American twentieth-century poetry that espoused clarity of language to encapsulate the essence of an image, moment or object. Imagist poets such as Ezra Pound, Amy Lowell (1874–1925) and T. E. Hulme (1883–1917) focused on the object, attempting to describe it in its purity or, as Pound called it, 'luminous details'.

If you wish to find out more about the lives and work of many of the writers mentioned in these Notes, *The Oxford Companion to English Literature*, edited by Margaret Drabble (sixth edition, 2000), is a good place to begin.

IMAGERY continued

CONTEXT

In 'Le Rire de la Méduse' ('The Laugh of Medusa', 1975) by Hélène Cixous (b.1937), the French feminist makes links between language, sexuality and the way we communicate. She draws attention to what she sees as a language that does not accommodate women's self-expression, and calls on women to create a feminine mode of writing: one that expresses the female body.

when Circe recalls herself 'breast-deep, in the sea, waving and calling' (34), we are again reminded of lost love.

There is much delight for the reader in Duffy's poetry, and presumably for Duffy too as the writer. This delight that Duffy expresses so abundantly is similar to 'jouissance'. The word translated means more than enjoyment, rather deep pleasure, and in literary theory refers to the bliss that relates to an intense experience – the 'Bliss' (29) perhaps that Queen Kong feels for her 'man' as she puts 'the tip of [her] tongue to the grape of his flesh' (28). It can also apply to the intense satisfaction that a writer or musician might feel in the completion of a difficult work. The French **feminists** have adopted the word to celebrate and express the **feminine** and the female body through laughter, sexuality, rhythm and music, seeing it as a type of female language. This, it seems, is what Duffy tries to do in *The World's Wife*. Her playfulness, the laughter, pensiveness and sometimes shock she evokes, and her celebration of the feminine and its eroticism, all come close to jouissance.

THE POWER OF THE TALE

CONTEXT

The English poet, novelist and scholar Robert Graves (1895–1985) wrote annotated versions of the Greek myths, which were published in two volumes as *The Greek Myths* (1955). He favoured a historical and anthropological approach to the understanding of myth.

The power of the tale is central to *The World's Wife*. Of the thirty poems in the collection, twenty are related to myth, fairy tale or biblical stories, and of the remaining poems some are linked to figures that are themselves connected to ancient tales. The giant gorilla of 'Queen Kong' takes its precedent from the modern myth *King Kong*, but also has links to the fairy tale 'Beauty and the Beast', while the Devil's wife's shocking involvement in child murder has parallels with the story of 'Little Red Riding Hood', where the child is at risk from the predatory wolf.

Stories such as myth, folk and fairy tale, legend and fable are continually being retold in different forms, and the battle between good and evil is still alive in popular culture. Carol Ann Duffy is by no means the only adult writer to be drawn to them. To understand the power of these tales we need to know something of their history and the effect they have on the human **psyche**. We have always told stories. Telling tales is an attempt to express and understand different aspects of life. The Greek myths, which have greatly influenced Western society, are **iconic** tales recorded in classical Greece around 500BC. They tell of gods, goddesses and Greek heroes, and involve supernatural elements, such as **transformation** from human to animal or creature. In *The World's Wife*, Medusa is a powerful transformation. Her portrayal as the 'foul mouthed … foul tongued, / yellow fanged' Gorgon (8–9) is tempered by her fearful backward glance at her lost beauty and youth.

In the mythical age of gods and men, humans and the gods coexist, though not usually happily. Myths often involve a dramatic encounter between a male god and a mortal woman, in which she is taken against her will, and from which a male hero is born. The myths are potent stories of conflict, love, lust, jealousy, revenge, birth and death, and they seem to appeal to latent desires and wishes, to human needs and impulses. For the psychoanalyst Sigmund Freud (1856–1939), myths were an expression of repressed thoughts, potentially recoverable through the interpretation of dreams. For the structural anthropologist Claude Lévi-Strauss (b.1908), myths, like language, have a common structure regardless of content or culture which link to thought processes deeply rooted in the brain.

Bruno Bettelheim (1903–90), a child psychologist, investigated fairy tales for their psychological meanings and their relevance to child development in *The Uses of Enchantment: The Meaning and Importance of Fairy Tales* (1976). In this work he discusses the fairy tale 'Beauty and the Beast'. For him it represents the vulnerable period before puberty. The burgeoning adolescent girl (Beauty) shifts her attachment from the father to the husband (the Beast) and overcomes fears of sexual intimacy. This is **symbolised** in her love for the Beast, which transforms him into a handsome prince. The tale also interests Duffy. Apart from its appearance in 'Queen Kong', it also occurs in the figure of Mrs Quasimodo, in the comparison between her and the beautiful gypsy girl, and of course in the poem 'Mrs Beast'. Duffy takes quite a different perspective from Bettelheim, however. There is nothing healing in her images. The Beast remains humiliated, demeaned; and for Mrs Quasimodo and her husband, there is no happy ending. The reader is left only

CONTEXT

Some of Freud's claims are now questioned, particularly by some feminists who see his depiction of women's sexuality as misjudged.

CHECK THE BOOK

Edmund Leach's book *Lévi-Strauss* (1970) is an excellent guide and includes a chapter entitled 'The Structure of Myth'.

CONTEXT

Carl Gustav Jung (1875–1961) was a Swiss psychiatrist and one-time colleague of Freud. In Jung's theory of the 'collective unconscious', part of the unconscious mind is shared by all humans regardless of culture. It reveals itself as symbols – **archetypes** – in areas such as myth, art and dreams.

CHECK THE BOOK

Walter Benjamin (1892–1940) in his essay 'The Storyteller', in *Illuminations* (a good edition is the 1999 translation by Harry Zohn), points out that the early folk tale would have contained something useful for the listener, perhaps a moral or some practical advice.

CHECK THE FILM

'Sapsorrow' is a version of 'Cinderella' in which Cinderella must marry her father the king after her mother's death. 'Sapsorrow' was an episode in the television series *The Storyteller* (1988), which was written by Anthony Minghella and produced by Jim Henson. A 1970 film, *Peau d'âne* (*Donkeyskin*), directed by Jacques Demy, has a striking image of Cinderella fleeing through the village dressed in a flowing cloak with the head of a donkey.

with the harrowing and moving image of Mrs Quasimodo, desperate in her rejected state, beyond consolation.

Originally, legends and fairy stories were oral tales, sometimes travellers' tales told from experience and embellished by the storyteller, and usually they were told in a communal setting. The story would then be passed on, and modified so that layers of meaning gave the story depth and resonance. This would be part of the cultural life of the community. Some tales might provide reassurance, but they could also include retribution for those who transgress, and therefore give us a glimpse of how grim and brutal life once was. In *The World's Wife* marriage and domestic life are often depicted in a modern context, and the woman is usually struggling to overcome her circumstances. 'Little Red-Cap' is a case in point. In a comment spoken by the wolf – 'How nice, breakfast in bed, he said' (26) – Duffy manages to conjure up the boredom of domesticity. It follows from previous more hopeful images – Little Red-Cap 'went in search of a living bird' (24) – and undermines Little Red-Cap's adolescent dreams, until finally she escapes from the wolf.

Ancient tales can also reveal how particular characters in domestic culture are formed – the wicked stepmother for example. One reason for her emergence is that women's early deaths, often in childbirth, meant male remarriage. The new wife and mother became the stereotypical cruel stepmother of fairy tales. In order to find a secure future, daughters would have to be married, and there was usually competition between daughters for dowry and husband. Stepmothers were therefore ambitious for their own daughters' progress in the quest for marriage. More disturbingly, however, such a character can deflect from a central issue in some tales. In 'Cinderella', a tale told across many cultures (the earliest recorded version goes back to the ninth-century Chinese), the hidden meaning is more shocking. Rather than neglect, sexual demands, usually from the father, drive the heroine into poverty and servitude. 'Cinderella' is in fact a tale of incest. Duffy no doubt is aware of this. In 'Mrs Beast', 'Ashputtel' (Cinderella) is among the 'line of ghosts / unable to win' (70–1). These ghosts are the abused female **icons** either from tales or history that Mrs Beast solemnly remembers and pays tribute to.

While the oral tradition still persisted in stories and ballads through the medieval period, the written word increasingly gained currency. This meant that the story could be more easily manipulated and controlled to suit certain **ideologies**. We cannot always trace the history of these tales, but we do know that at times they were sanitised. In other words, the stories were rewritten so as not to offend the audience reading them. This was in fact normal practice in the seventeenth and eighteenth centuries. Jacob and Wilhelm Grimm, the Brothers Grimm, are probably the best-known compilers of what were assumed to be the original peasant folk tales. But the extent to which the Grimms edited and rewrote them is greater than might be supposed. Jack Zipes claims that they collected their tales not from the peasantry but from the aspiring early nineteenth-century middle classes, who themselves had made modifications. Indeed, the Grimms, aware of their audience, often changed the stories to meet demand. For example, the emphasis given to the role of the dutiful daughter is apparent in the rewriting of 'Snow White'. In the Grimms' 1810 collection she was obliged only to cook for the dwarfs. By the 1812 edition she must 'sew, make the beds, wash and knit and keep everything tidy and clean' and 'in the evening dinner must be ready' as well.

It is clear that legends, myths and fairy tales are not only wonderfully creative flights of the imagination but have deep resonances in our culture. The magic and **symbolism** of the tales, together with the clearly delineated gender roles they support, provide Duffy with much to develop and equally much to 'put ... straight' ('Mrs Beast', 2).

Revisionism

Revisionism, in literature, is the rewriting or retelling of a story so that various features are altered. Characters and their motivations are usually changed in order to convey a different message or meaning from the well-known tale. These stories cover myths, fairy or folk tales, religious stories and **narratives** that have become embedded in the culture, such as *Frankenstein* or *King Kong*. They may also include historical figures.

CHECK THE NET

Find references to the following versions of 'Cinderella' at **www.wikipedia.org**: 'Fair', 'Brown and Trembling', 'Finette Cendron', 'Cap O'Rushes', 'Catskin', 'Allerleirauh', and 'Katie Woodencloak'.

CHECK THE BOOK

Routledge's 2002 edition *Complete Fairy Tales* includes every one of the two hundred and ten tales collected by Jacob and Wilhelm Grimm.

CHECK THE BOOK

In *Breaking the Magic Spell: Radical Theories of Folk and Fairy Tales* (first published 1979; second revised edition 2002) Zipes discusses the folk- and fairy-tale genre and its historical development, challenging many psychological readings.

CHECK THE BOOK

In *Feminism and Poetry: Language, Experience, Identity in Women's Writing* (1987) Janet Montefiore draws attention to the ubiquity of fairy tale and myth in women's poetry, providing other examples taken at random.

CONTEXT

Anne Sexton's *Transformations* retells seventeen Brothers Grimm tales. In so doing she questions many of the conventional ideas related to femininity found in the tales.

CHECK THE BOOK

Ostriker's concept of 'revisionist mythmaking' is discussed in 'The Thieves of Language: Women Poets and Revisionist Mythmaking'. This essay can be found in *The New Feminist Criticism: Essays on Women, Literature and Theory*, edited by Elaine Showalter (1985).

There is now an established tradition of these **revisions** among women writers, Angela Carter's *The Bloody Chamber and Other Stories* (1979) being among the most highly regarded. The speaker of such tales is a female voice, and while the plot often remains intact, the mood serious or comic, the images **lyrical** or bawdy, **irony** is usually involved. Traditionally these tales are an attempt to articulate female experience in a masculine world, to challenge norms and explain things 'as they really are'. This is done by changing or undermining female **archetypes** that are also stereotypes: the virginal daughter, the wicked stepmother, the siren – the women in Greek mythology who lure sailors to their doom. It is an attempt to throw off a masculine definition and misrepresentation of femininity and discover a new one. The revision of fairy tales and myths is a common enterprise in women's poetry. References to them abound. A poem may contain a single image from a myth or tale; or a complete volume, such as *The World's Wife*, may be given over to rewritings. Similarly, the poets Liz Lochhead (*The Grimm Sisters*, 1981) and Anne Sexton (*Transformations*, 1971) have devoted whole collections to the task.

Women are not the only ones who rewrite myths and tales, but it does seem to preoccupy many at some point in their writing, including, of course, Duffy. During the 1980s Alicia Ostriker described this as 'revisionist mythmaking' and highlighted the search for a separate female identity outside masculine definition as the single greatest preoccupation among women poets since the 1960s. Challenging these assumptions and received meanings through poetry would seem on the face of it to be a useful way forward. After all, poetry has the capacity to heighten the sensations, to create powerful **imagery** and set language in relief. Often the speaker is **foregrounded**. Duffy's use of the **dramatic monologue** presents the reader with an articulate, persuasive voice.

But there are difficulties with this approach. Telling 'things as they really are' is not as easy as it seems, particularly through poetry. For poetry of all the arts is especially fictive and has many layers of meaning. For example, Queen Kong, the female counterpart of King Kong, is a comic but powerful figure. She has fallen in love with a man from a documentary team who has come to make a film about a species of toad on the island. She takes over his life and when he dies she has him preserved, 'with tiny emeralds for eyes' (line 75), and strung around her neck. So he becomes a necklace. Or is he a totem and she the alpha male? A Freudian reading might investigate that. A **feminist** reading might say that he is a doll, powerless and subjugated, and play up the irony. There are other **connotations** that any reader might make. This is because we can play with meaning in the poem. It is not fixed. Although we might agree on a range of preferred readings, there is no guarantee that other inferences will not be drawn by other readers.

CHECK THE BOOK

In *The Handless Maiden* (1994) the poet Vicki Feaver (b.1943) includes the poem 'Circe'. It is useful to compare this with Duffy's poem 'Circe' in *The World's Wife.*

Another dilemma for women rewriting lies in the use of the strong voice, whether through the use of the dramatic monologue, as in the case of *The World's Wife*, or through a storyteller figure. By demanding a position, the **feminine** voice is certainly heard. It is authoritative and commanding – and here lies the dilemma. By aligning itself with authority (or the masterful), it must in part be defined by **patriarchy**. There is yet another difficulty when women poets attempt to depict female experience as it is lived. Whose experience are they depicting? Women's lives are varied and depend on a whole series of factors as well as gender: class, race, sexuality, age and chance. And finally, mythic tales themselves are potent. Their potency derives in part from deeply embedded cultural and historical processes (see **The power of the tale**). As significant **symbols** some have existed within culture and patriarchy for millennia and are not easy to undermine or exorcise.

CHECK THE BOOK

Silences (first published in 1978) by Tillie Olsen (1912–2007) includes an investigation on the difficulties faced by women writers. Olsen discovered that all the great Western women writers up to the late twentieth century either had no children or had someone, such as a nanny, to help raise their offspring. Olsen has been enormously influential in the women's movement.

There would seem then to be insurmountable problems in finding a female writing identity. However, Carol Ann Duffy finds her own way to engage with myths and fairy tales. Well aware of the pitfalls, she explores female identity from a variety of perspectives. In *The World's Wife* she uses a multitude of voices to convey female experience. The women of these poems are not victims. They are usually in control of their circumstances. And she is not afraid to explore the darker side of the female **psyche**, as evidenced in the depiction of Myra Hindley in 'The Devil's Wife', for example. She is also aware of the limits of dealing with language, of its inability to say what we mean, of that common experience of being 'lost for words'. Some of her poems in other collections deal directly with the problems language presents. In 'Words, Wide Night' (*The Other Country*) she comments: 'This is pleasurable. Or shall I cross that out and say / it is sad?' In *The World's Wife* she draws on all aspects of language, such as slang, insult, **colloquialism**, its **lyricism** and its sound.

Nor in *The World's Wife* does Duffy remain faithful to the traditional outcomes of the original tale, so her characters, with one or two exceptions (Medusa, for example), are not trapped. In Anne Sexton's acclaimed *Transformations* (1971), there is a single female voice, a **narrator**, who introduces and relates familiar fairy tales: 'The speaker in this case / is a middle-aged witch, me –' The broad effect is to produce an exposé of female experience while simultaneously remaining faithful to the genre. They are bleak tales where the characters, female in particular, are caught up in a world that is damaging, pernicious even, and where outcomes are inevitable, beyond change: 'Cinderella and the prince / lived, they say, happily ever after, / … their darling smiles pasted on for eternity.'

By contrast, *The World's Wife* is no respecter of tradition. Pygmalion's bride rids herself of her unwanted husband and announces triumphantly: 'And [I] haven't seen him since. / Simple as that' (50–1); Eurydice fools Orpheus so that he vanishes instead of her: 'I waved once and was gone' (109); and Little Red-Cap escapes from the wolf by her own efforts: 'Out of the forest I come with my flowers, singing, all alone' (42). In this way Duffy not only exposes the female stereotype, she turns it on its head so the female is empowered. And, as we have seen, the plots change. Sometimes there is only a tenuous link to the original story, and yet she still draws on the mythic power of the tale. This is a critical point. Duffy can be said to be creating something new, her own poetry of female experience, not simply a **revision** of an old tale, and by doing this her imagination is given free rein.

CONTEXT

Women poets who revisit fairy tale and myth include Stevie Smith ('The Frog Prince' and 'Persephone' in her 1978 *Selected Poems*); Lesley Saunders ('Klytemnestra'); Libby Houston ('Introduction to an Old Story' in her 1981 volume *At the Mercy*); and Fleur Adcock ('The Ex-Queen Among the Astronomers' in her 1983 *Selected Poems*). As early as 1982, Duffy herself created an image around Hans Christian Andersen's 'The Princess and the Pea' in her poem 'Gestures', published in *Fifth Last Song*.

PART FOUR

CRITICAL HISTORY

CRITICAL RECEPTION

Carol Ann Duffy is a popular poet. The publication of *The World's Wife* (1999) brought her to the notice of the ordinary book-buying public, and in the first year it sold over five thousand copies. By 2002 the sales had reached tens of thousands. This is rare for a volume of poetry, and remarkable for a contemporary one. Her popularity has been compared to that of Philip Larkin during the 1960s. Though well respected, prior to this Duffy was largely known in academic circles and on the poetry circuit, where she has been established since her days with the Liverpool poets in the 1970s. With the popular success of *The World's Wife* her profile changed and gave her greater access to mainstream publishers.

The publication of *The World's Wife* attracted media interest. This was coupled with speculation that Duffy might be appointed to the post of Poet Laureate in the same year (see **Historical and political background**). Regular interviews with Duffy were conducted at this time in the daily press, again an unusual occurrence for a poet. Katharine Viner in an interview at the time of publication wrote:

> The World's Wife is her most overtly feminist work, and I ask if it was her primary intention to give voice to women denied a say in the past. 'I think the poems are looking for the missing truth, rather than accepting the way we've been taught.'
>
> ('Metre Maid', *Guardian*, 25 September 1999)

The critic Sean O'Brien, quoted in the same article, called her 'the representative poet of her day'. Though most critics value her work, not all do. Simon Brittan is one, and regards her work as 'simplistic language and overstated imagery' (for a fuller critique see 'Language and Structure in the Poetry of Carol Ann Duffy' in *Thumbscrew*, 1:1, winter 1994–5, pp. 58–64). Helen Dunmore reviewed Duffy's 1998 work *The Pamphlet*, in which Duffy included 'Mrs Icarus', noting that 'the joke can wear thin, and in

CONTEXT

Philip Larkin (1922–85) is considered to be among the most influential English poets of the twentieth century. *The Whitsun Weddings* (1964) and *High Windows* (1974) are two of his collections.

WWW. CHECK THE NET

Duffy discusses her life and work and the creation of *The World's Wife* in an interview with Katharine Viner, published in the *Guardian* on 25 September 1999. To read this lengthy article entitled 'Metre Maid', go to **www.guardian.co.uk** and search for Viner and 'Metre Maid'.

CHECK THE BOOK

Sean O'Brien's *The Deregulated Muse: Essay on Contemporary British and Irish Poetry* (1998) offers a fine commentary on Duffy and many other contemporary poets.

CONTEXT
Eileen Atkins, Jill Balcon and Elizabeth Bell have recorded *The World's Wife* as an audiobook (1999).

Duffy's case it doesn't seem the best use for her talent. The talent is so apparent … that any falling off is the more disappointing' ('Waiting for *The World's Wife*', *Poetry Review*, 89:2, summer 1999). As Dunmore acknowledges, poems such as 'Mrs Icarus' work better in performance, where they are well received. It should also be remembered that Duffy's intention is partly to appeal to the ordinary person as well as to those in literary circles.

Duffy has received many awards during her writing career (see **Carol Ann Duffy's life and works**), and *The World's Wife* was shortlisted for the Forward Poetry Prize in the year it was published – the same year that she became a Fellow of the Royal Society of Literature.

CONTEMPORARY APPROACHES

In the late twentieth and early twenty-first centuries critical approaches to literature have been dominated by the **postmodernist** movements: **structuralism** and **post-structuralism**, including **deconstruction**. They all move away from the idea of a stable meaning in the text, the approach that governed the nineteenth-century reading of literary works. Running in parallel with postmodernism and sometimes part of it are **Marxism**, **feminism**, **post-colonialism** and **psychoanalytic** approaches. A text can be read in a variety of ways. However, in the current academic climate a preferred reading of a text is more likely to be decided by the kind of text under focus. For example *The World's Wife* would suggest a feminist reading that might also draw on other approaches, such as deconstruction and psychoanalysis.

CHECK THE BOOK
For a scholarly work on the female literary tradition, see *Literary Women* (1976) by Ellen Moers (1929–79).

FEMINIST LITERARY CRITICISM

Feminist literary criticism covers several critical practices, but broadly speaking it applies feminist theory to the study of texts in an attempt to understand and challenge representations of women. Feminist critics have long been interested in how these representations conform to stereotypical ideas about what it is to be a woman. In challenging these stereotypes, which are many and sometimes conflicting, they see them as socially, culturally and psychologically constructed. In other words they are deeply held concepts, so deeply embedded that men and women regard them as inherent female traits. In addition, the values attached to these assumptions have led to inequalities between the sexes, and rigid definitions of gender. *The World's Wife* challenges many of these assumptions and inequalities by creating a variety of complex female speakers who do not subscribe to conventional ideas about women. Sometimes feminine and masculine stereotypes are conflated, and this is often where the **irony** and humour lies. Mrs Beast and her coterie behave like male chauvinists: 'On my Poker nights, the Beast / kept out of sight' (47–8). The Kray sisters are modelled on two alpha male figures, the Kray twins, one of whom was gay, the other bisexual. Queen Kong, who has the physique of the male gorilla King Kong, is stereotypically feminine: 'Next day, I shopped. Clothes for my man, mainly, / but one or two treats for myself from Bloomingdale's' (55–6). Duffy uses the technique in non-humorous poems too. Salome, while clearly a woman, has the attributes of a serial killer, a figure usually associated with men; and Pope Joan is a female in what is a male-only world in reality. In *The World's Wife* Duffy exposes conventional ideas of gender and sexuality, as well as exploring female inequality.

Some feminist critics, namely the French feminists who are also post-structuralists – Hélène Cixous, Luce Irigaray and Julia Kristeva – go further, seeing language as a masculine **construct** that excludes female experience. Cixous coined the term '*écriture féminine*'. Literally it means 'women writing', but is also what she calls 'writing the body', a liberating writing practice. 'Writing the body' is perceived as a means by which a writer can become free from masculine language and definition. For Cixous and other French feminists, language and sexuality are bound together and masculine discourse cannot accommodate female experience; it is too rigid and controlled. Female expression is free-flowing, Cixous claims, and non-linear. We could compare it to the writing technique stream of consciousness – a stream of continuous disordered thoughts. The voice expressed in a literary work is therefore characteristically in a state of movement or flux.

CONTEXT

Cixous (b.1937), Irigaray (b.1930) and Kristeva (b.1941) belong to the post-structuralist feminist movement and see links between sexuality and language. They seek to create a **feminine discourse** and depart from what they see is the dominant masculine one. They are influenced by the French psychoanalyst Jacques Lacan (1901–81).

CONTEXT

Virginia Woolf (1882–1941) is one of the best-known exponents of the stream of consciousness method (*Mrs Dalloway*, 1925 and *To the Lighthouse*, 1927). Another is James Joyce (1882–1941) in his novels *Ulysses* (1922) and *Finnegans Wake* (1939).

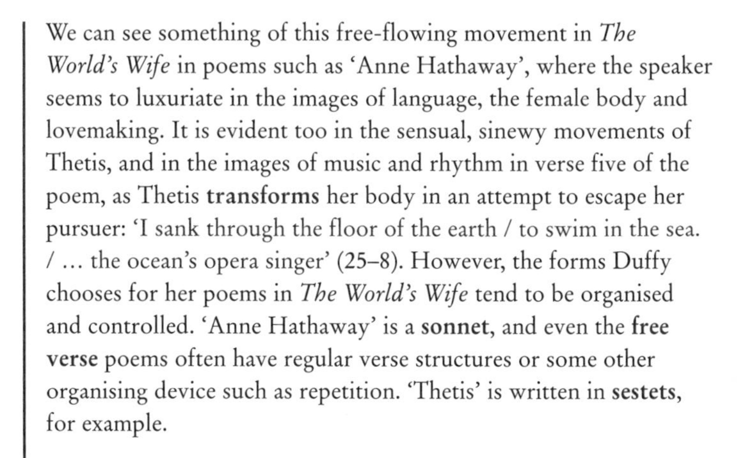

We can see something of this free-flowing movement in *The World's Wife* in poems such as 'Anne Hathaway', where the speaker seems to luxuriate in the images of language, the female body and lovemaking. It is evident too in the sensual, sinewy movements of Thetis, and in the images of music and rhythm in verse five of the poem, as Thetis **transforms** her body in an attempt to escape her pursuer: 'I sank through the floor of the earth / to swim in the sea. / ... the ocean's opera singer' (25–8). However, the forms Duffy chooses for her poems in *The World's Wife* tend to be organised and controlled. 'Anne Hathaway' is a **sonnet**, and even the **free verse** poems often have regular verse structures or some other organising device such as repetition. 'Thetis' is written in **sestets**, for example.

CHECK THE BOOK

Rees-Jones' excellent study of '*from* Mrs Tiresias' in her book *Consorting with Angels: Essays on Modern Women Poets* (2005) explores gender and the body and Tiresias' attitude to his sexuality (pp.160–2).

One poem in which Duffy explores issues of gender and the body more fully and also engages with **deconstruction** is '*from* Mrs Tiresias'. Deryn Rees-Jones, discussing how Duffy plays with Tiresias' dual sexuality, says:

> Mrs Tiresias sees Duffy addressing explicitly the relationship between gender and the body, exploring the performances that make up gender, and also, potentially, deconstructing them.
>
> (*Consorting with Angels: Essays on Modern Women Poets*, 2005, p. 160)

Deconstruction can appeal to **feminists** because it sees meaning as rooted in culture and society and is focused on the way texts undercut the attempt to find structure in a work. In Duffy's exploration of Tiresias, his gender and sexuality become increasingly unstable as we read the poem. Tiresias is first a man, then a woman, but retains his masculine qualities, unable to accept his new self. This repression is manifest in his awkward relationship with his body and his discomfort with sexuality and sex. Although he inhabits a woman's body, we are reminded, as Rees-Jones says, of a man 'in drag'. At the end of the poem Tiresias faces his wife's new female lover and Duffy draws parallels between the two as though they were, in the last lines, mirror images of each other: 'his hands, her hands, / the clash of their sparkling rings and their painted nails' (92–3). We are left uncertain about what Duffy is saying about gender. Rees-Jones calls on Judith Butler to elaborate:

'In this twist Duffy seems to be suggesting that all gender is, as Judith Butler has argued, "an act … a performance that is repeated … a re-enactment and re-experiencing of a set of meanings already socially established"' (*Consorting with Angels: Essays on Modern Women Poets*, p. 161; Rees-Jones quotes from Butler's *Gender Trouble: Feminism and the Subversion of Identity*, p. 140).

But perhaps this very uncertainty is Duffy's point. Deconstruction takes apart the text to see what its underlying meanings, ideas and cultural and social assumptions are, and in so doing sees those very meanings slip away. A definition of meaning can therefore never be complete.

PSYCHOANALYTIC CRITICISM

Psychoanalytic theories are theories of the unconscious, originally developed by Sigmund Freud (1856–1939). The unconscious is that part of our mental functioning of which we are unaware, and which contains suppressed desires, memories and anxieties. These can be expressed in dreams. It is easy therefore to see how poetry and works of art in general, which are fictive in nature and part of the imagination, can be linked to psychoanalysis. A critical approach adopting Freud's theories would search for expressions of unconscious desires or repressed thoughts. Freud indeed sees the creation of art in therapeutic terms. Sublimation, the act of channelling negative feelings into more acceptable or positive expression, is for him exemplified in the artistic process. In Duffy's poem 'Penelope' the speaker channels her longing for her absent lover into creativity. Circe might be said, albeit with a sense of humour, to do much the same in terms of cuisine and recipes for pig.

The unconscious can also emerge through jokes, **double meanings** and slips of the tongue: Freudian slips. From this point of view alone, *The World's Wife* would encourage psychoanalytic criticism, in its use of **puns** and wordplay. There are other ways too in which it might inspire such a reading. Freud drew on several Greek myths to explore his ideas and to validate them. In the images expressed by Eurydice there is a clear sense of Thanatos, the death instinct. She is only too happy to find herself 'dead and down / in the

CHECK THE BOOK

Judith Butler (b.1956) is an American philosopher, post-structuralist and feminist. Her book *Gender Trouble: Feminism and the Subversion of Identity* (1990) was a popular bestseller. In it she suggests ways in which gender and sexuality are culturally constructed.

CHECK THE BOOK

A useful book that helps with the understanding of literary theory is *Literary Theory: A Very Short Introduction* by Jonathan Culler (1997).

CONTEXT

Thanatos is the **personification** of Death in Greek mythology, the son of Nyx (Night) and the brother of Hypnos (Sleep).

CONTEXT

The Swiss linguist Ferdinand de Saussure (1857–1913) proposed that language is made up of a system of signs. A sign is something that stands for something else (for example the word 'chair' stands for the 'thing that we sit on'). The word 'chair' is the signifier and 'thing that we sit on' is the signified. But there is nothing implicit in the signifier 'chair' that gives a clue to its meaning. Saussure's ideas led to the development of **semiotics**, which examines signs in such fields as literary theory, psychology and anthropology. His ideas had a large impact on **structuralism** and **post-structuralism**.

Underworld, a shade' (1–2), to be away from the world and be free of her husband. In Freudian terms Thanatos is a desire expressed by all of us, a desire to return to a state of peace or non-being. One poem that lends itself to Freudian critical analysis is 'The Devil's Wife', perhaps most vividly in the third part, 'Bible'. The speaker appears to be in a state of denial about her involvement in child murder. This denial for Freud would be a defence mechanism. It is a way of distancing a reality that threatens the ego or the conscious self. In 'The Devil's Wife' the reader hears the disturbing repetitions and monotone rhythm of the speaker's voice as Duffy cleverly suggests the wife's ego has been fragmented.

Some **feminists** quarrel with Freud's theories, particularly those concerned with the development of the girl child. They see his theories, especially that of penis envy, as largely privileging the male. Freud suggests that part of a girl's successful psychological development into womanhood depends on her unconscious acceptance that she lacks a penis. In 'Frau Freud' Duffy plays with the theory, empowering her speaker so that envy is replaced by pity. Some feminists largely accept Freud's views, noting that he was an early supporter of women's rights. Others partially accept them, while introducing their own ideas. One notable feminist Shulamith Firestone (b.1945) suggests that it is the power of the masculine world that women envy, and succinctly replaces 'penis envy' with 'power envy'.

The French psychoanalyst Jacques Lacan (1901–81) has heavily influenced the work of the French feminists. He takes Freud's theories of the unconscious and applies them to language, looking at the development of the infant before language has been acquired, and how the self begins to develop. As the child develops, so these imaginary identifications build, and passing through other stages of development the child constructs what is a sense of self that seems whole, but is divided between the conscious ego and unconscious desires. Language is similar and related, according to Lacan. There is always a gap between the signifier and the signified, between the words we use and their meanings and between language and reality. We can never fully say what we mean.

In this context a **psychoanalytic** reading of *The World's Wife* might focus on the way that Duffy uses the **dramatic monologue**, a primary device in each poem. The voice is certain and reliable. There are moments when we question the reliability of the speaker, for example in 'The Devil's Wife' and again in 'Queen Kong', where the gigantic speaker sees herself as discreet and unobtrusive. But for the most part the voice is **foregrounded** and strong so that the identity of the speaker seems to be whole, stable and undifferentiated. A psychoanalytic reading might explore the way such a voice is an illusion, a trick played on us by the language of the text.

Course in General Linguistics by Ferdinand de Saussure, translated by Roy Harris (1995), is a fine introduction to this linguist's work.

PART FIVE

BACKGROUND

CONTEXT

Fleshweathercock and Other Poems was published in 1974. In an interview with Katharine Viner Duffy claimed to be embarrassed by the publication, calling it 'a mixture of Keats and Sylvia Plath and Dylan Thomas and the Bible. A sort of teenage mix' ('Metre Maid', *Guardian*, 25 September 1999).

CHECK THE NET

Ambit is an influential and non-profit-making arts magazine established in 1959, supported by the Arts Council. It promotes the work of new writers and artists. Go to **www.ambit magazine.co.uk** for more information.

CAROL ANN DUFFY'S LIFE AND WORKS

Born in Glasgow on 23 December 1955 to Mary and Frank Duffy, Carol Ann Duffy was the eldest child and only girl in a Roman Catholic family. Her mother was Irish and her father's family had Irish origins. When Duffy was six the family moved to Stafford, where she attended St Austin's Roman Catholic Primary School followed by St Joseph's Convent and later Stafford Girls' High School. She grew up in a working-class community. Frank Duffy was a shop steward and a Labour councillor. Both Catholicism – which Duffy rejected, as she did all religion – and politics are apparent in her work.

Duffy seems to have had a strong writing identity from an early age, showing promise at primary school, where she was encouraged to write by her teachers, and this continued into secondary school. Her first pamphlet of poems, *Fleshweathercock and Other Poems*, was published by Outposts when she was only eighteen. She also met the older poet and artist Adrian Henri, one of the Liverpool poets, who became her mentor and with whom she lived for several years. She studied philosophy at Liverpool University from 1974 to 1977. After graduation she worked for Granada Television, and in the 1980s moved to London, initially working as a writer in residence in East End schools. She also worked as a freelance writer and began a long-standing association with the influential poetry magazine *Ambit* as a poetry editor. Between 1988 and 1989 she was the *Guardian* poetry critic.

Duffy has written plays as well as poetry: *Take My Husband* (1982), *Cavern of Dreams* (1984), *Little Women, Big Boys* (1986), and a radio play, *Loss* (1986). Her plays have been performed at the Liverpool Playhouse and the Almeida Theatre, and she adapted her collection of *Grimm Tales*, working with Tim Supple, who dramatised them for performance at the Young Vic in 1996 and 1997. In 1996 she moved from London to settle in Manchester, where she lectures at the Writing School, home to a postgraduate course in creative and academic writing. Apart from *The World's Wife*, published in 1999, Duffy's other major adult collections of poetry include *Standing Female Nude* (1985), *Selling Manhattan* (1987), *The Other Country* (1990), *Mean Time* (1993), *Feminine Gospels* (2002) and *Rapture* (2005). Penguin published her *Selected Poems* in 1994, and in 2004 Picador published her *New Selected Poems 1984–2004*.

Her first major award, of which she has many, was a C. Day Lewis Fellowship in 1982. She received the Somerset Maugham Award in 1988 for *Selling Manhattan* and the Dylan Thomas Award in 1989. Other prestigious awards include the Scottish Arts Council Book Award for *Standing Female Nude*, and for *The Other Country* in 1990 and again in 1993 for *Mean Time*. This last volume also won the Forward Poetry Prize, Best Poetry Collection of the Year, and the Whitbread Poetry Award in 1993. A Lannan Literary Award in 1995 granted her a teaching post at Wake Forest University in North Carolina, and in the same year she was awarded the OBE. Duffy has had relationships with both women and men; her daughter, Ella, whose father is the writer Peter Benson, was born in 1995. In 1999 Duffy was made a Fellow of the Royal Society of Literature. Duffy also writes for children, and was shortlisted for the Whitbread Children's Book Award in 2000 for *Meeting Midnight*. This was followed in 2001 by a five-year fellowship by the National Endowment of Science, Technology and the Arts (NESTA), and in 2005 she received the T. S. Eliot Prize, awarded for *Rapture* (2005).

HISTORICAL AND POLITICAL BACKGROUND

Carol Ann Duffy was brought up in the 1950s and 1960s in what she has described to Katharine Viner as 'a loving, strict, happy Catholic household: holidays in Blackpool every summer' ('Metre Maid', *Guardian*, 25 September 1999). Although women were very much part of the post-war labour force at this time, the locus of women's lives was largely domestic, and many had lost the independence they had known during the war. Most had done traditional male jobs as part of the war effort, reflected in women's militaristic fashions of the 1940s. Conversely, the fifties saw small waists and high heels come into vogue.

CHECK THE NET

Peter Forbes in 'Winning Lines', an article published in the *Guardian* on 31 August 2002, provides a useful account of Duffy's life and work, including her early experiences as a poet in Liverpool. Visit **www.guardian.co.uk** and search for 'Winning Lines Forbes Duffy'.

CHECK THE BOOK

For a discussion of Duffy's writing for a younger audience, read Eva Müller-Zettelmann's essay '"Skeleton, Moon, Poet": Carol Ann Duffy's postmodern poetry for children' in *The Poetry of Carol Ann Duffy: 'Choosing Tough Words'*, edited by Angelica Michelis and Antony Rowland (2003).

CHECK THE BOOK

Michael Schmidt's *Lives of the Poets* (1998) is an accessible study that helps to place Duffy and her contemporaries in context.

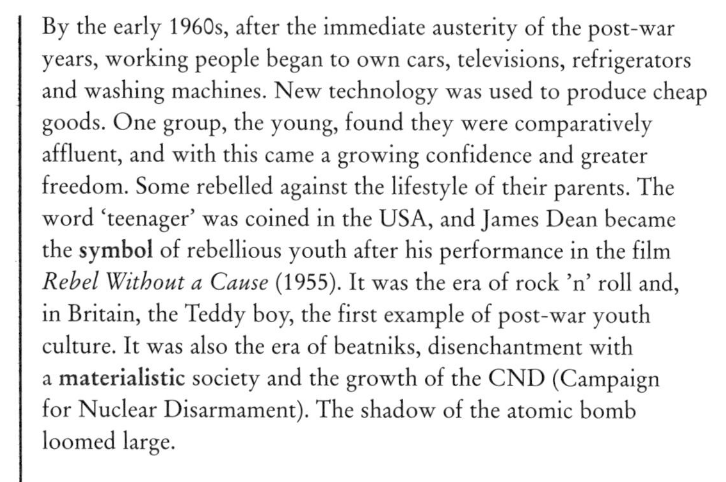

By the early 1960s, after the immediate austerity of the post-war years, working people began to own cars, televisions, refrigerators and washing machines. New technology was used to produce cheap goods. One group, the young, found they were comparatively affluent, and with this came a growing confidence and greater freedom. Some rebelled against the lifestyle of their parents. The word 'teenager' was coined in the USA, and James Dean became the **symbol** of rebellious youth after his performance in the film *Rebel Without a Cause* (1955). It was the era of rock 'n' roll and, in Britain, the Teddy boy, the first example of post-war youth culture. It was also the era of beatniks, disenchantment with a **materialistic** society and the growth of the CND (Campaign for Nuclear Disarmament). The shadow of the atomic bomb loomed large.

CHECK THE BOOK

Jake Arnott's acclaimed trilogy, which opens with *The Long Firm* (1999), is set in the London underworld of the 1960s, similar to that of the Kray twins, who are referred to by name in the novels.

The 1960s was the period in which the Kray twins, the inspiration for Duffy's poem 'The Kray Sisters', dominated gangland London. The 'swinging sixties' have become synonymous in the popular imagination with the Beatles, a booming economy and a permissive society. There was an expansion in university education, and it was a time of activism among students, who felt able to challenge the values of their parents. But it was also a time of poverty, prejudice and poor housing. Ken Loach's *Cathy Come Home*, broadcast in 1966 and an early example of the drama-documentary, charts the decline and breakdown of a young family unable to find decent, affordable accommodation. The programme had such an impact on the watching public that there was an outcry, and it gave impetus to the formation of the charity Shelter. Duffy's own concern with the dispossessed or the abused would be reflected later in poems such as 'Lizzie, Six' and 'Education for Leisure' (*Standing Female Nude*).

CHECK THE FILM

Willy Russell (b.1947) wrote the well-known play *Educating Rita* in 1980. It was made into a film in 1983, directed by Lewis Gilbert and starring Julie Walters, Michael Caine and Maureen Lipman.

By the early 1970s the teenage Duffy had entered the poetry circuit in Liverpool and become acquainted with the Liverpool poets. In the 1960s Liverpool was famous for its popular culture; it was the home of 'the Mersey Sound', the Beatles and also a flourishing poetry scene. When Duffy went to university there in 1974 she became very much part of the cultural life of the city, where she met the playwrights Alan Bleasdale and Willy Russell, with whom she became friends. *Fifth Last Song* was written in collaboration with Liverpool painters, and her early plays were performed at the Liverpool Playhouse in the early 1980s. Later, too, Duffy would write 'Liverpool Echo' (*Standing Female Nude*) in remembrance of the city and its heyday.

The 1970s also saw conflict in Northern Ireland. British mainland troops had been sent there in 1969, and in 1972 thirteen people in Belfast were killed during a civil rights march on what became known as Bloody Sunday. The IRA retaliated by bombing Aldermaston barracks, in which five died. Duffy would write the poem 'War Photographer' (*Standing Female Nude*) in which Belfast is listed and in which she contrasts the experience of the photographer and what he records through the lens of his camera with the version presented to the public through the media.

As the 1970s progressed, the radical student movements of the sixties gave way to single-issue politics and pressure groups such as animal rights and gay liberation. The women's movement had begun to gather momentum in the sixties, entering what is sometimes known as second-wave **feminism**, which continued through much of the 1980s. The 1970s began with a landmark publication: Germaine Greer's *The Female Eunuch*. Duffy's feminism no doubt developed during these decades, when the 'personal' was seen as 'political'. In other words, feminists saw their relationships and domestic lives as a political arena, as well as focusing on inequalities in the wider society. Lesbian feminism also became more overt at this time, as lesbian and gay politics became visibly concerned with rights and inequalities. Most of the poems in *The World's Wife* explore women's relationships with men but also include those that celebrate women's relationships with each other.

When Margaret Thatcher became the first woman prime minister in 1979, it signalled a move to the right in British politics, a distinct shift away from a welfare state to a market economy. Thatcher was also determined to limit trade union power. Duffy, an anti-Thatcherite, would have been acutely aware of these issues. Her father, a trade unionist, stood as a candidate for the Labour Party during the 1980s, and Duffy herself wrote a poem for the

CONTEXT

The television dramatist and playwright Alan Bleasdale (b.1946) wrote *Boys from the Blackstuff* in 1982, about unemployment. This television series, broadcast in five episodes, established him as a leading dramatist of social and political issues.

CHECK THE BOOK

In *The Female Eunuch* (first published in 1970) Greer argues that the nuclear family subjugates and represses women, divorcing them from their sexuality, limiting their sphere of action and reducing them to 'eunuchs'.

Trade Union Conference in September 1999. Thatcherism focused on individualism. Young people growing up in the 1980s and 1990s, assumed to be influenced by Thatcherism, were often seen as avaricious and **materialistic** by the media and referred to as the 'me' or the 'greed' generation. The term 'yuppie' was also coined, an elaboration of the acronym from 'young urban professional'. The youthful Fausts of *The World's Wife* possess such values, and 'Mrs Faust' can be seen as a **satire** on late twentieth-century capitalism. Certainly large sums of money were made on the stock market as the economy boomed. Duffy, a poet conscious of social and political issues, wrote her volume *The Other Country* at this time, in which she included poems such as 'Making Money'.

CONTEXT

The Poet Laureate is a poet officially appointed by the government, and is expected to write poems for state occasions. In 1999 the Laureateship was awarded to Andrew Motion (b.1952).

By the 1990s Carol Ann Duffy was a well-established poet and had won many awards, and in 1999 it was rumoured that she would become the next Poet Laureate. But a minor controversy over her suitability for the post on account of her lesbianism was played out in the press and apparently became the concern of the prime minister, Tony Blair. Katharine Viner notes in her interview 'Metre Maid' (published on 25 September 1999 in the *Guardian*) that a Downing Street official commented on the concerns that the prime minister had about a homosexual poet becoming Poet Laureate, since it might trouble the mainstream right-wing voter. In the event Duffy did not get the award, although she makes clear in the same interview that had she been offered the Laureateship, it is unlikely that she would have accepted. *The World's Wife* was published in the same year and went on to become her most popular volume.

LITERARY BACKGROUND

Carol Ann Duffy came to public notice very early in her writing career and has gone through several changes as a poet. In her youth John Keats (1795–1821) was an influence, and she seems to have used him as a model in some of her first experiments. Robert Browning (1812–89) as the earliest proponent of the **dramatic monologue** must be another. *The World's Wife* is also reminiscent of Geoffrey Chaucer (*c.*1342–1400) and the collected voices of his pilgrims telling *The Canterbury Tales*.

Duffy's relationship with Adrian Henri and her experience of poetry readings with the popular Liverpool poets in the 1970s will also have informed her work and no doubt her interest in performance and contact with the public. Henri, a painter as well as a poet, practised photorealism and pop art. He was also interested in surrealism, and the visuals arts are specifically referred to in Duffy's work, though not in *The World's Wife* to any degree.

It is generally accepted by most critics that Duffy's main influences are **feminism** and modernism. The former is self-evident in *The World's Wife*, and there are several women poets, and prose writers such as Angela Carter, whose influences are apparent in the volume, largely because Duffy follows a female tradition in the rewriting of myth and tale (see also **Reading *The World's Wife*** and **The power of the tale** for a discussion of these influences). However, one of the greatest influences on the collection is the major American poet Adrienne Rich (b.1929). She comes from an older generation than Duffy but, like her, she began writing early, received early public recognition and has received numerous awards. She has been actively involved in the women's movement for many years; she is a more overtly political poet than Duffy – she describes herself as a political poet – and sees her poetry as directly addressing feminist issues. Her style is **lyrical**, but while there are lyrical moments in *The World's Wife*, this is not the principal area of influence. This lies in Duffy's concern to challenge female stereotypes and in her exploration of female identity. Rich's volume of poetry *The Dream of a Common Language: Poems 1974–1977* (1978) is concerned with female creativity identity and the search for a female **discourse**. Several of the figures in *The World's Wife* are concerned with this (see the **Detailed summaries** for 'Little Red-Cap' and 'Penelope').

Modernism is the other major influence on Carol Ann Duffy's poetry. It was a powerful movement that began to emerge before the First World War and gained impetus after it, partly in response to the carnage and brutality and the loss of faith in a benign world, but also in response to the changing economic and political climate. It has its roots in the nineteenth century, when in philosophy, the arts and science certainties such as religious faith were being questioned. In poetry this questioning reaches its most powerful expression in the

CONTEXT

The Liverpool Poets was the name given to a group of three poets, Adrian Henri (1932–2000), Roger McGough (b.1937) and Brian Patten (b.1946), who used the fame of Liverpool as a centre of youth culture during the era of the Beatles to promote their work by giving it a group identity. They performed and published their work together.

CHECK THE BOOK

The Mersey Sound: Penguin Modern Poets 10 (1967), an anthology by Henri, McGough and Patten, has been one of the all-time bestselling volumes of poetry.

CONTEXT

Duffy can also be linked to a tradition of other women writers as diverse as Toni Morrison (b.1931) Michèle Roberts (b.1949), Jeanette Winterson (b.1959) and Zadie Smith (b.1975), who are all feminist influenced.

CONTEXT

Arnold's 'Dover Beach' is often referred to for its depiction of the crisis of faith felt during Victorian times. Arnold provides a link between romanticism and modernism.

CHECK THE BOOK

Simone de Beauvoir's *The Second Sex* (1949) is a seminal work on feminism. Her work on existentialism, *The Ethics of Ambiguity* (1947), explains the concept more easily than Sartre's *Being and Nothingness* (1943).

CONTEXT

Justin Quinn (b.1968) is an Irish poet and critic. He has published several collections, including *Waves and Trees* in 2006.

poem 'Dover Beach' (1867) by Matthew Arnold (1822–88). Modernism encompassed a wide range of fields including art, architecture, music, philosophy, literature and literary theory. In France the writer Jean-Paul Sartre (1905–80) developed the philosophy of **existentialism**. Humanity is seen as existing within a meaningless universe and freedom comes through an acknowledgement of this, and recognising that we and not fate are responsible for our actions. His partner, Simone de Beauvoir (1908–86), was a **feminist**. She also explored existentialism, as did other French writers such as Albert Camus (1913–60). They are all part of modernism.

The leading modernist poets were Ezra Pound (1885–1972) and T. S. Eliot (1886–1965), and the latter has had a special influence on Duffy. There are several ways in which her poetry is similar, and in *The World's Wife* this is most evident in the use of **colloquialism** and **cliché** and the **dramatic monologue**. In an interview with Andrew McAllister, Duffy commented: 'If I had to pick one who devastated me and made me shiver … still it would be Eliot' (*Bête Noire*, 6, winter 1988). Neil Roberts in his essay 'Duffy, Eliot and impersonality' (in *The Poetry of Carol Ann Duffy: 'Choosing Tough Words'*, edited by Angelica Michelis and Antony Rowland, 2003) notes the similarity between Duffy's work and T. S. Eliot's, and acknowledges that although *The World's Wife* is the least 'Eliot-like' of her volumes, the influence is still clearly there. Eliot's influence is also discussed earlier in the **Detailed summaries** for 'Queen Herod', where a comparison is drawn between the poem and T. S. Eliot's 'The Journey of the Magi' (1927). Note, however, that Roberts regards Duffy's poem as more of a riposte than a homage.

We would not immediately associate Duffy with Philip Larkin, and Duffy has remarked that she sees no similarities at all. But critics would argue that poets are not necessarily the best judge of their own work. At times their poems do seem to coincide, for example in their use of colloquialism, their likeness for form and rhyme and in their accessibility (Justin Quinn has noted that their themes can also be similar). And from time to time even in *The World's Wife*, a particularly lively and wicked volume, there is a touch of Larkin's melancholy here and there. A useful comparison is the depiction of the suburban landscape in the opening of 'Little Red-Cap' with a similar depiction in the opening lines of Larkin's 'Afternoons' (published in his 1964 collection *The Whitsun Weddings*).

World events	Carol Ann Duffy's life	Literary events
1955 Winston Churchill resigns as prime minister and is replaced by Anthony Eden; Ruth Ellis is the last woman to be hanged in Britain	**1955** Born on 23 December in Glasgow	**1955** Adrienne Rich, *The Diamond Cutters and Other Poems*
1958 Campaign for Nuclear Disarmament (CND) formed; first London to Aldermaston protest march		**1958** Simone de Beauvoir, *Memoirs of a Dutiful Daughter*
1963 President John Kennedy assassinated; Harold Macmillan resigns as prime minister after Profumo scandal; 'Beatlemania' in Britain		**1963** Betty Friedan, *The Feminine Mystique*; Sylvia Plath dies
1964 Labour win the general election; Harold Wilson becomes prime minister		
		1965 Sylvia Plath, *Ariel*
		1967 Denise Levertov, *The Sorrow Dance*
1968 Martin Luther King assassinated; Anti-Vietnam War demonstrations in Grosvenor Square, London		
		1969 Stevie Smith, *The Frog Prince*
		1970 Germaine Greer, *The Female Eunuch*; Kate Millett, *Sexual Politics*
		1971 Anne Sexton, *Transformations*; Stevie Smith dies

World events	Carol Ann Duffy's life	Literary events
1972 Civil unrest; Bloody Sunday shootings in Northern Ireland		
1973 Britain joins European Economic Community (EEC)		
1974 President Richard Nixon resigns over Watergate scandal	**1974** *Fleshweathercock and Other Poems* **1974–7** Attends Liverpool University	**1974** Shere Hite, *Sexual Honesty: By Women for Women*; Anne Sexton dies
1975 Fall of Saigon; American troops withdraw from Vietnam		
		1978 Adrienne Rich, *The Dream of a Common Language: Poems 1974–1977*; Anne Sexton, *Words for Dr Y*; Stevie Smith, *Selected Poems*
1979 Tories win general election; Margaret Thatcher becomes prime minister		**1979** Angela Carter, *The Bloody Chamber and Other Stories*
		1980 Elaine Feinstein, *The Feast of Eurydice*; Frances Horovitz, *Water over Stone*
1981 Ronald Reagan becomes US president; mass protests at Greenham Common against nuclear cruise missiles		**1981** Liz Lochhead, *The Grimm Sisters*; Sylvia Plath, *Collected Poems*
1982 Falklands War	**1982** *Fifth Last Song*; *Take My Husband* (play); awarded C. Day Lewis Fellowship	

World events	Carol Ann Duffy's life	Literary events
	1983 'Whoever She Was' wins National Poetry Competition	**1983** Grace Nichols, *I Is a Long Memoried Woman*; Carol Rumens, *Star Whisper*; William Golding wins Nobel Prize for Literature
1984 Miners' strike; IRA bomb at Conservative Party Conference, Brighton; Indira Gandhi, Indian prime minister, assassinated	**1984** *Cavern of Dreams* (play); wins Eric Gregory Award	**1984** Ted Hughes becomes Poet Laureate
	1985 *Standing Female Nude*	**1985** Gillian Clarke, *Selected Poems*
1986 Accident at Chernobyl nuclear power station, Ukraine	**1986** *Thrown Voices*; *Little Women, Big Boys* (play); *Loss* (radio play); wins Scottish Arts Council Book Award for *Standing Female Nude*	**1986** Wendy Cope, *Making Cocoa for Kingsley Amis*; Michèle Roberts, *The Mirror of the Mother: Selected Poems 1975–1985*; Simone de Beauvoir dies; Charles Causley receives CBE
1987 International stock market crash known as Black Monday	**1987** *Selling Manhattan*	
	1988 Somerset Maugham Award for *Selling Manhattan*	
1989 Berlin Wall dismantled; Tiananmen Square protests and killings in China	**1989** Dylan Thomas Award	
1990 Demonstrations against poll tax; Margaret Thatcher resigns; John Major becomes prime minister	**1990** *The Other Country* published and wins Scottish Arts Council Book Award	

World events	Carol Ann Duffy's life	Literary events
1991 Gulf War; break-up of Soviet Union		**1991** Angela Carter, *Wise Children*; Jackie Kay, *The Adoption Papers*
1992 Conservatives re-elected	**1992** *William and the Ex-Prime Minister*; *I Wouldn't Thank You for a Valentine* (editor); wins Cholmondeley Award	**1992** Tony Harrison, *The Gaze of the Gorgon*; Jo Shapcott, *Phrase Book*; Derek Walcott wins Nobel Prize for Literature; Angela Carter dies
1993 Bill Clinton becomes US president	**1993** *Mean Time* published and receives Forward Poetry Prize, Whitbread Poetry Award and Scottish Arts Council Book Award	**1993** Moniza Alvi, *The Country at My Shoulder*; Jackie Kay, *Other Lovers*; Toni Morrison wins Nobel Prize for Literature
1994 Civil war in Rwanda; Channel Tunnel opens	**1994** *Selected Poems*; *Anvil New Poets 2*	**1994** Vicki Feaver, *The Handless Maiden*
	1995 *Penguin Modern Poets 2*; Lannan Literary Award; takes up teaching post at Wake Forest University, North Carolina; receives OBE; daughter, Ella, born	**1995** Seamus Heaney wins Nobel Prize for Literature
	1996 *Grimm Tales* (adapted with Tim Supple); *Stopping for Death* (editor)	
1997 New Labour wins general election; Tony Blair becomes prime minister	**1997** *More Grimm Tales*; Signal Poetry Award for *Stopping for Death*	**1997** Fleur Adcock, *Looking Back*; Ted Hughes, *Tale from Ovid*; Denise Levertov dies

World events	Carol Ann Duffy's life	Literary events
	1998 *The Pamphlet*	**1998** Ted Hughes' *Birthday Letters* wins Forward Poetry Prize, T. S. Eliot Prize and Whitbread Book of the Year; Ted Hughes dies
1999 Kosovo crisis	**1999** *The World's Wife*; *Meeting Midnight* published and shortlisted for Whitbread Children's Book Award; *Five Finger Piglets* with Brian Patten, Roger McGough, Jackie Kay, Gareth Owen and Peter Bailey; *Time's Tidings* (editor); made a Fellow of the Royal Society of Literature	**1999** Simon Armitage, *Killing Time*; Seamus Heaney's *Beowulf* wins Whitbread Book of the Year; Andrew Motion becomes Poet Laureate
	2000 *The Oldest Girl in the World*; awarded five-year fellowship by National Endowment of Science, Technology and the Arts (NESTA)	**2000** U. A. Fanthorpe, *Consequences*; Mimi Khalvati, *Selected Poems*; Anne Stevenson, *Granny Scarecrow*; Grace Nichols receives Cholmondeley Award; Adrian Henri dies
2001 New Labour re-elected; George W. Bush becomes US president; terrorist attack on World Trade Center	**2001** *Hand in Hand* (editor); awarded CBE	**2001** Eavan Boland, *Against Love Poetry*; Seamus Heaney, *Electric Light*; Paul Muldoon, *Poems 1968–1998*; Selima Hill's *Bunny* wins Whitbread Prize; V. S. Naipaul wins Nobel Prize for Literature; Michael Longley receives Queen's Gold Medal for Poetry

World events	Carol Ann Duffy's life	Literary events
2002 Introduction of euro in twelve European countries	2002 *Feminine Gospels*; *Queen Munch and Queen Nibble* (illustrated by Lydia Monks); *Underwater Farmyard* (illustrated by Joel Stewart)	2002 Brian Patten receives Cholmondeley Award and the Freedom of the City of Liverpool
2003 Second Gulf War	2003 *The Good Child's Guide to Rock 'n' Roll*; *Collected Grimm Tales*	2003 Roger McGough, *Collected Poems*; Don Paterson's *Landing Light* receives T. S. Eliot Prize
2004 Tsunami disaster in South East Asia	2004 *New Selected Poems 1984–2004*; *Out of Fashion: An Anthology of Poems* (editor); *Overheard on a Saltmarsh: Poets' Favourite Poems* (editor)	2004 Elizabeth Bartlett, *Mrs Perkins and Oedipus*; Kate Clanchy, *Newborn*; Kathleen Jamie, *The Tree House*
2005 Terrorist attacks in London	2005 *Rapture* published and awarded T. S. Eliot Prize; *Another Night Before Christmas*; *Moon Zoo*	2005 Harold Pinter wins Nobel Prize for Literature
	2006 *The Lost Happy Endings* (illustrated by Jane Ray)	2006 Simon Armitage, *Tyrannosaurus Rex Versus the Corduroy Kid*; Vicki Feaver, *The Book of Blood*; Seamus Heaney's *District and Circle* wins T. S. Eliot Prize

FURTHER READING

Peter Ackroyd, *Shakespeare: The Biography*, Chatto & Windus, 2005

Aesop, *The Complete Fables*, translated by Olivia and Robert Temple, Penguin, 1998

Simone de Beauvoir, *The Second Sex*, Vintage edition, 1989

Walter Benjamin, 'The Storyteller', in *Illuminations*, translated by Harry Zohn and introduced by Hannah Arendt, Pimlico, 1999

John Berger, *Ways of Seeing*, Penguin, 1972 (reprinted 1990)

Bruno Bettelheim, *The Uses of Enchantment: The Meaning and Importance of Fairy Tales*, Vintage edition, 1989

Eavan Boland, *Object Lessons: The Life of the Woman and the Poet in Our Time*, Carcanet, 1995

Simon Brittan, 'Language and Structure in the Poetry of Carol Ann Duffy', *Thumbscrew*, 1:1, winter 1994–5, pp. 58–64

Judith Butler, *Gender Trouble: Feminism and the Subversion of Identity*, Routledge, 1990

Angela Carter, *The Bloody Chamber and Other Stories*, Vintage edition, 2006

Jonathan Culler, *Literary Theory: A Very Short Introduction*, Oxford University Press, 1997

Jane Dowson and Alice Entwistle, *A History of Twentieth-Century British Women's Poetry*, Cambridge University Press, 2005

Margaret Drabble (ed.), *The Oxford Companion to English Literature*, Oxford University Press, sixth edition, 2000

Helen Dunmore, 'Waiting for *The World's Wife*', *Poetry Review*, 89:2, summer 1999

Terry Eagleton, *Literary Theory: An Introduction*, University of Minnesota Press, 1983 (revised edition, 1996)

Peter Forbes, 'Winning Lines', *Guardian*, 31 August 2002

Marilyn French, *The Women's Room*, Virago edition, 2007

FURTHER READING

Betty Friedan, *The Feminine Mystique*, with an introduction by Anna Quindlen, W. W. Norton edition, 2001

Lucy Gent (ed.), *Albion's Classicism: Visual Arts in England, 1550–1660*, Yale University Press, 1995

Sandra M. Gilbert and Susan Gubar, *The Madwoman in the Attic: The Woman Writer and the Nineteenth-Century Literary Imagination*, Yale University Press, 1979

Sandra M. Gilbert and Susan Gubar (eds.), *Shakespeare's Sisters: Feminist Essays on Women Poets*, Indiana University Press, 1981

Robert Graves, *The Greek Myths*, Penguin, 1955 (revised edition, 1993)

Germaine Greer, *The Whole Woman*, Anchor Books edition, 2000

Germaine Greer, *The Female Eunuch*, Farrar, Straus and Giroux edition, 2001

Jacob and Wilhelm Grimm, *The Complete Fairy Tales*, Routledge edition, 2002

Park Honan, *Shakespeare: A Life*, Clarendon Press, 1998

Cora Kaplan, *Salt and Bitter and Good: Three Centuries of English and American Women Poets*, Paddington Press, 1975

Edmund Leach, *Lévi-Strauss*, Collins, 1970

Andrew McAllister, 'Carol Ann Duffy Interview', *Bête Noire*, 6, winter 1988, pp. 69–77

Angelica Michelis and Antony Rowland (eds.), *The Poetry of Carol Ann Duffy: 'Choosing Tough Words'*, Manchester University Press, 2003

Ellen Moers, *Literary Women*, Doubleday, 1976

Janet Montefiore, *Feminism and Poetry: Language, Experience and Identity in Women's Writing*, Pandora, 1987

Janet Montefiore, *Arguments of Heart and Mind: Selected Essays 1977–2000*, Manchester University Press, 2002

FURTHER READING

Janet Montefiore, 'Feminism and the Poetic Tradition', *Feminist Review*, 13, spring 1983

Christopher Norris, *Deconstruction: Theory and Practice*, Routledge edition, 1991

Sean O'Brien, *The Deregulated Muse: Essays on Contemporary British and Irish Poetry*, Bloodaxe, 1998

Tillie Olsen, *Silences*, The Feminist Press, 2003

Alicia Ostriker, 'The Thieves of Language: Women Poets and Revisionist Mythmaking' in *The New Feminist Criticism: Essays on Women, Literature and Theory*, edited by Elaine Showalter, Pantheon, 1985

John Pearson, *The Profession of Violence: The Rise and Fall of the Kray Twins*, HarperCollins, revised edition, 1995

Deryn Rees-Jones, *Carol Ann Duffy*, Northcote House, 2001

Deryn Rees-Jones, *Consorting with Angels: Essays on Modern Women Poets*, Bloodaxe, 2005

Adrienne Rich, *The Dream of a Common Language: Poems 1974–1977*, W. W. Norton, 1978

Adrienne Rich, *Collected Early Poems 1950–1970*, W. W. Norton, 1993

Madan Sarup, *An Introductory Guide to Post-Structuralism and Postmodernism*, University of Georgia, 1993

Ferdinand de Saussure, *Course in General Linguistics*, translated by Roy Harris, Duckworth, 1995

Michael Schmidt, *Lives of the Poets*, Wiedenfield & Nicholson, 1998

Maria Tatar, *The Classic Fairy Tales*, W. W. Norton, 1998

Katharine Viner, 'Metre Maid', *Guardian*, 25 September 1999

Jack Zipes, *Fairy Tales and the Art of Subversion*, Routledge edition, 1991

Jack Zipes, *Breaking the Magic Spell: Radical Theories of Folk and Fairy Tales*, University Press of Kentucky, revised edition, 2002

Literary terms

alliteration the repetition of the same consonant in a stretch of language, most often at the beginnings of words or on stressed syllables

allusion a passing reference in a work of literature to something outside the text; may include other works of literature, myth, historical facts or biographical detail

alter ego a second self, or second **persona** within a person

anaphora in poetry the repetition of the same word or words at the beginning of lines to create poetic effects

antithesis the placing together of contrasting ideas usually to create balance

archetype in literature a recurring **symbol** or **motif** often with its roots in myth. In psychoanalysis these are symbols of the unconscious that have primitive origins

assonance the use of the same vowel sound with different consonants or the same consonant with different vowel sounds in successive words or stressed syllables in a line of verse

blank verse unrhymed **iambic pentameter**

cadence the recurring rise and fall of the rhythms of speech. Can also refer to a rhythm that comes at the close of a line or poem

caesura a pause during a line of poetry

cantos short divisions of a long poem

cautionary tale a story that warns of danger, usually with a moral. Typically the character disobeys a warning or is incautious and comes to an unfortunate end

cliché a widely used expression which, through overuse, has lost impact and originality

closed couplet a **couplet** that is usually rhymed and contains an entire thought

colloquial the everyday speech used by people in informal situations

conceit an extended or elaborate concept that forges an unexpected connection between two apparently dissimilar things

connotation an idea or feeling implied by words, beyond the literal meaning

consonance repeated arrangements of consonants, with a change in the vowel that separates them, for example slip / slop, lump / limp / lamp

construct a model or concept

couplet a pair of rhymed lines of any **metre**

deconstruction in literary theory, a **post-structuralist** approach in which a text is unpicked and meanings sought, only to find that meanings shift and complicate

dipodic a light rocking **metre** of two feet (a unit of rhythm)

discourse a formal written or spoken communication or debate. Used in literary theory to refer to a particular kind of debate or reasoning, as in 'feminist discourse'

doggerel verse that is trite or sentimental or has a forced rhythm. Sometimes used by poets purposely to create comic effects

double entendre a **double meaning**; sometimes with a crude **connotation**

double meaning a figure of speech in which meaning can be understood in two ways

double rhyme in which two final syllables rhyme: d*ouble* tr*ouble*

dramatic monologue a poetic form in which a single voice addresses the reader at any one time, creating a strong sense of personality. A poem may contain more than one voice, or voices in unison

elegy a formal poem lamenting a death or written in sorrowful mood

end rhyme rhyme at the end of lines of poetry

end stop a pause at the end of a line of poetry

enjambment in poetry when a line runs on into the next line, without pause, so carrying the thought with it. See also **run-on line**

epigraph a quotation or comment at the beginning of a poem or other work, relevant to the theme or content

euphemism an inoffensive word or phrase substituted for one considered offensive or harmful

existentialism a philosophical approach, in which the individual can only be free by acknowledging their illogical position in a meaningless universe. It is an anti-religious philosophy. The individual is a free agent, who governs their own development through their own will

feminine the term, when used in literary theory, particularly **feminism**, refers to the socially and culturally constructed woman

feminine rhyme an unaccented syllable at the end of a line of poetry, for example walking / talking

feminism a range of movements seeking equality for women socially, politically, economically and culturally

figurative when language is used in an non-literal way, for example a literary device such as **metaphor**

foregrounded a literary term used to point to a feature of the text that is accentuated, such as the **narrator**

free verse verse without a metrical pattern; may contain some rhyme

full rhyme when the vowel and consonant in words rhyme, for example June / moon

gender politics a politics concerned with the significance of gender at a social, cultural and psychological level

Gothic in literature a style that includes horror and the supernatural, popular in the eighteenth century

Grand Guignol short play depicting violence and horror popular in Parisian cabarets in the nineteenth and early twentieth centuries, mainly at the Théâtre du Grand Guignol

hyperbole deliberate exaggeration, used for effect (from the Greek for 'throwing too far')

iambic pentameter a line of poetry consisting of five iambic feet (iambic consisting of a weak syllable followed by a strong one)

icon in popular culture a famous person or image that embodies certain qualities

ideology a belief system or system of ideas

imagery descriptive language which uses images to make actions, objects and characters more vivid in the reader's mind. **Metaphors** and **similes** are examples of imagery

imperative direct request or command

insult poem a comic poem that pokes fun at someone, using exaggeration

internal rhyme when words rhyme in the middle and at the end of a line

intertextuality the explicit or implicit referencing of other texts within a work of literature. It is designed to put the work within the context of other literary works and traditions and implies parallels between them

irony the humorous or sarcastic use of words to imply the opposite of what they normally mean; incongruity between what might be expected and what actually happens; the ill-timed arrival of an event that had been hoped for

juxtaposition contrasting ideas that are placed together

lyric poetry, complex or simple, that expresses the emotions and thoughts of the speaker, often exploring a single feeling or idea

Marxism the political and economic theories of Karl Marx (1818–83) and Friedrich Engels (1820–95). In Marxism the class struggle is the basic force behind historical change. The economic conditions of a period determine or profoundly influence the political, social and cultural **ideology**. Marxist literary criticism is concerned with the relationship between the historical conditions and the ideology expressed in literature and which produces the work

materialism in philosophy the idea that nothing exists except the material world and its shifts or changes, as opposed, for example, to religious or spiritual belief (**Marxism** is a materialist theory)

metaphor a figure of speech in which a word or phrase is applied to an object, a character or an action which does not literally belong to it, in order to imply a resemblance and create an unusual or striking image in the reader's mind

metre the rhythmic arrangement of syllables in poetic verse

misogyny a dislike or hatred of women

motif a recurring idea in a work, which is used to draw the reader's attention to a particular theme or topic

narrative story, tale or any recital of events, and the manner in which it is told

narrator the voice telling the story or relating the sequence of events

objectify to treat people as objects rather than as individual human beings. Women, for example, may be treated as sex objects, in which sexual characteristics are the focus. Objectification is an important issue in **feminism**

parody an imitation of a work of literature or a literary style designed to ridicule the original

pastiche a work in a style or manner that imitates that of another work; when deliberate, it may be a form of **parody**

pathos the power of arousing feelings of pity and sorrow in a work

patriarchy a social system in which masculine values and power dominate

performance poem a poem written to be presented to an audience, rather than read privately

persona in literature the voice of the speaker or **narrator**, not the author's voice, presenting a point of view

personification the treatment or description of an object or an idea as human, with human attributes and feelings

Petrarchan sonnet sonnet that has an *abba abba* rhyme scheme followed by a **sestet** *cdcdcd* or other rhyme patterns; also known as an Italian sonnet. See also **sonnet**

phallocentric used in **feminism** to refer to the dominance of masculine values

post-colonialism philosophical and literary approaches that study the aftermath of colonial rule, usually looking at texts and issues that focus on cultural identity as a result of or after colonisation

postmodernism a radical movement that gained ground in the late twentieth century, postmodernism overlaps many fields of study. In literary criticism a text is viewed as open to a plurality of meaning and form. Uncertainty rather than a fixed perspective is a key feature of postmodernism

post-structuralism an approach that questions many of the assumptions inherent in **structuralism**, seeing meanings as fluid and unstable

protagonist the principal character in a work of literature

psyche in psychoanalysis, the self. Can also refer to the human mind or spirit. In Greek mythology Psyche is the mortal woman with whom Eros falls in love

psychoanalytic criticism in literature, applying an approach to understanding a text by analysing the unconscious motivations of, for example, the characters

pun similar to a word with a **double meaning**, a pun plays with two or more meanings in a word. Most often used for comic effect

quatrain four lines of verse. Can stand alone or be a repeating form in a poem

quintain five lines of verse. Can stand alone or be a repeating form in a poem

rap in popular culture, a monologue with a strong rhythm and rhyme performed with musical backing

register styles of speech used in different social situations

revisionism in literature the rewriting of a well-known text in which character and/or plot is changed in order to challenge the view presented in the original

rhetoric the art of persuasive speaking or writing. A rhetorical question is asked for effect rather than to elicit an answer

rhyming couplet two lines of poetry, usually the same length, that rhyme

run-on line see **enjambment**

satire a type of literature in which folly, evil or topical issues are held up to scorn through ridicule, **irony** or exaggeration

semiotics the study of human communication through signs, **symbols** and groups of signs (such as words) and their relationship to meaning

sestet a verse of six lines

Shakespearean sonnet a sonnet that has an *abab cdcd efef gg* rhyme scheme. See also **sonnet**

simile a figure of speech in which one thing is compared to another using 'like' or 'as'

slant rhyme rhyme which is not exact and where the vowel is different: tomb / time. Sometimes called half rhyme or off rhyme

socialisation learning the values, attitudes and customs of a society through family, school and other social groups, to the extent that these values are accepted as true

soliloquy a dramatic device which allows a character to speak as if thinking aloud, revealing their inner thoughts, feelings and intentions

sonnet a fourteen-line verse which includes a **rhyming couplet** at the end, written in **iambic pentameter**. See also **Shakespearean sonnet** and **Petrarchan sonnet**

stanza traditional verse that has a fixed number of lines and a rhyme scheme that is repeated

structuralism in literary theory a way of analysing a text for its underlying deeper elements or structure and its relationship to other texts of a similar structure, rather than examining, for example, the features and effects of character or the **narrative** voice. Structural theories are evident in a variety of fields such as linguistics, the social sciences and the humanities

subtext an underlying theme or idea in a literary work

symbolism investing material objects with abstract powers and meanings greater than their own; allowing a complex idea to be represented by a single object

synonym a word that means the same or nearly the same as another word

tercet a verse of three lines, sometimes rhymed

timbre in literature the quality of the voice or tone

tragedy in its original sense, a drama dealing with elevated actions and emotions and characters of high social standing in which a terrible outcome becomes inevitable as a result of an unstoppable sequence of events and a fatal flaw in the personality of the **protagonist**. More recently, tragedy has come to include courses of events happening to ordinary individuals that are inevitable because of social and cultural conditions or natural disasters

transformation in myth and folklore the physical change of a human, animal, plant or inanimate object. In the fairy tale 'Beauty and the Beast', for example, the beast is transformed into a man

vernacular regional speech

vers libre see **free verse**

Author of these notes

Mary Green has an MA in Language, Arts and Education from the University of Sussex and is a well-established educational author. She has written over a hundred books, many of them in the fields of English and the humanities, and has carried out research into women's writing. She also writes fiction, poetry and picture books for children.

York Notes for GCSE and Key Stage 3

GCSE

Maya Angelou
I Know Why the Caged Bird Sings

Jane Austen
Pride and Prejudice

Alan Ayckbourn
Absent Friends

Elizabeth Barrett Browning
Selected Poems

Robert Bolt
A Man for All Seasons

Harold Brighouse
Hobson's Choice

Charlotte Brontë
Jane Eyre

Emily Brontë
Wuthering Heights

Brian Clark
Whose Life is it Anyway?

Robert Cormier
Heroes

Shelagh Delaney
A Taste of Honey

Charles Dickens
David Copperfield
Great Expectations
Hard Times
Oliver Twist
Selected Stories

Roddy Doyle
Paddy Clarke Ha Ha Ha

George Eliot
Silas Marner
The Mill on the Floss

Anne Frank
The Diary of a Young Girl

William Golding
Lord of the Flies

Oliver Goldsmith
She Stoops to Conquer

Willis Hall
The Long and the Short and the Tall

Thomas Hardy
Far from the Madding Crowd
The Mayor of Casterbridge
Tess of the d'Urbervilles
The Withered Arm and other Wessex Tales

L. P. Hartley
The Go-Between

Seamus Heaney
Selected Poems

Susan Hill
I'm the King of the Castle

Barry Hines
A Kestrel for a Knave

Louise Lawrence
Children of the Dust

Harper Lee
To Kill a Mockingbird

Laurie Lee
Cider with Rosie

Arthur Miller
The Crucible
A View from the Bridge

Robert O'Brien
Z for Zachariah

Frank O'Connor
My Oedipus Complex and Other Stories

George Orwell
Animal Farm

J.B. Priestley
An Inspector Calls
When We Are Married

Willy Russell
Educating Rita
Our Day Out

J. D. Salinger
The Catcher in the Rye

William Shakespeare
Henry IV Part I
Henry V
Julius Caesar
Macbeth
The Merchant of Venice
A Midsummer Night's Dream
Much Ado About Nothing
Romeo and Juliet
The Tempest
Twelfth Night

George Bernard Shaw
Pygmalion

Mary Shelley
Frankenstein

R.C. Sherriff
Journey's End

Rukshana Smith
Salt on the snow

John Steinbeck
Of Mice and Men

Robert Louis Stevenson
Dr Jekyll and Mr Hyde

Jonathan Swift
Gulliver's Travels

Robert Swindells
Daz 4 Zoe

Mildred D. Taylor
Roll of Thunder, Hear My Cry

Mark Twain
Huckleberry Finn

James Watson
Talking in Whispers

Edith Wharton
Ethan Frome

William Wordsworth
Selected Poems

A Choice of Poets

Mystery Stories of the Nineteenth Century including The Signalman

Nineteenth Century Short Stories

Poetry of the First World War

Six Women Poets

For the AQA Anthology:

Duffy and Armitage & Pre-1914 Poetry

Heaney and Clarke & Pre-1914 Poetry

Poems from Different Cultures

Key Stage 3

William Shakespeare
Henry V
Macbeth
Much Ado About Nothing
Richard III
The Tempest

YORK NOTES ADVANCED

Margaret Atwood
Cat's Eye
The Handmaid's Tale

Jane Austen
Emma
Mansfield Park
Persuasion
Pride and Prejudice
Sense and Sensibility

William Blake
Songs of Innocence and of Experience

Charlotte Brontë
Jane Eyre
Villette

Emily Brontë
Wuthering Heights

Angela Carter
Nights at the Circus
Wise Children

Geoffrey Chaucer
The Franklin's Prologue and Tale
The Merchant's Prologue and Tale
The Miller's Prologue and Tale
The Prologue to the Canterbury Tales
The Wife of Bath's Prologue and Tale

Samuel Coleridge
Selected Poems

Joseph Conrad
Heart of Darkness

Daniel Defoe
Moll Flanders

Charles Dickens
Bleak House
Great Expectations
Hard Times

Emily Dickinson
Selected Poems

John Donne
Selected Poems

Carol Ann Duffy
Selected Poems
The World's Wife

George Eliot
Middlemarch
The Mill on the Floss

T. S. Eliot
Selected Poems
The Waste Land

F. Scott Fitzgerald
The Great Gatsby

John Ford
'Tis Pity She's a Whore

E. M. Forster
A Passage to India

Michael Frayn
Spies

Charles Frazier
Cold Mountain

Brian Friel
Making History
Translations

William Golding
The Spire

Thomas Hardy
Jude the Obscure
The Mayor of Casterbridge
The Return of the Native
Selected Poems
Tess of the d'Urbervilles

Seamus Heaney
Selected Poems from 'Opened Ground'

Nathaniel Hawthorne
The Scarlet Letter

Homer
The Iliad
The Odyssey

Aldous Huxley
Brave New World

Kazuo Ishiguro
The Remains of the Day

Ben Jonson
The Alchemist

James Joyce
Dubliners

John Keats
Selected Poems

Philip Larkin
High Windows
The Whitsun Weddings and Selected Poems

Christopher Marlowe
Doctor Faustus
Edward II

Ian McEwan
Atonement

Arthur Miller
All My Sons
Death of a Salesman

John Milton
Paradise Lost Books I & II

Toni Morrison
Beloved

George Orwell
Nineteen Eighty-Four

Sylvia Plath
Selected Poems

William Shakespeare
Antony and Cleopatra
As You Like It
Hamlet
Henry IV Part I
King Lear
Macbeth
Measure for Measure
The Merchant of Venice
A Midsummer Night's Dream
Much Ado About Nothing
Othello
Richard II
Richard III
Romeo and Juliet
The Taming of the Shrew
The Tempest
Twelfth Night
The Winter's Tale

Mary Shelley
Frankenstein

Richard Brinsley Sheridan
The School for Scandal

Bram Stoker
Dracula

Jonathan Swift
Gulliver's Travels and A Modest Proposal

Alfred Tennyson
Selected Poems

Alice Walker
The Color Purple

Oscar Wilde
The Importance of Being Earnest
A Woman of No Importance

Tennessee Williams
Cat on a Hot Tin Roof
The Glass Menagerie
A Streetcar Named Desire

Jeanette Winterson
Oranges Are Not the Only Fruit

John Webster
The Duchess of Malfi

Virginia Woolf
To the Lighthouse

William Wordsworth
The Prelude and Selected Poems

W. B. Yeats
Selected Poems